A VERY PRIVATE GENERAL

A VERY PRIVATE GENERAL

A biography of
General Frederick Coutts,
CBE, Hon DD (Aberdeen)

Ronald Thomlinson

International Headquarters of The Salvation Army
101 Queen Victoria Street, London EC4P 4EP

Copyright © 1990 The General of The Salvation Army
First published 1990
ISBN 0 85412 566 3

MAJOR RONALD THOMLINSON
became a Salvation Army officer in 1968 and has served
in corps, training college and divisional headquarters
appointments. Between 1973-79 he was on the staff of
the Editorial Department, International Headquarters,
and has since been an editor in the Netherlands before
taking his present appointment as a divisional commander
in that territory.

Cover by Jim Moss

Printed in Great Britain by
The Campfield Press, St Albans

Acknowledgments

It would have been quite impossible to write a biography about such a private person as General Coutts without the help of many people around the world who took the trouble to record their contacts with him and make them available for publication. I am also grateful to several territories which gave time, material and finance to this project. In particular a word of appreciation must be expressed to the Netherlands Territory which accepted the largest share of the costs and has supported me in the realisation of this book.—R. T.

Preface

Frederick Coutts was the sort of man who generated stories, and the anecdotes about him are legion. He was so unique that when these stories were recounted, the teller usually adopted a 'Coutts' posture, sentence construction and mannerisms. But even to those who would claim to have known him best, he remained a mystery. He was constantly working and, even whilst in the company of others, spent many hours alone with his thoughts; he did not easily allow people into his personal world. This book is therefore an attempt to show just what kind of man Frederick Coutts was, and what the circumstances were in his life which, apart from his natural character and talents, may have moulded him into the sort of person he became. His ability to communicate to the masses was, it seems, in inverse proportion to his ability to communicate in the smaller informal setting.

Many with whom he had worked or who had been influenced by him were reluctant to acknowledge his weaknesses, but he does not need that kind of protection: he was too great a man for that. Besides, it would be an insult to his memory to make of this biography a hagiography: he had read and written too much himself and was too wise and honest a man to receive that kind of treatment. This book must contain the same integrity as he possessed in life.

Ronald Thomlinson
Rotterdam 1989

Note. The rank given to officers in this story is the one held by them at the time of reference.

And to think that it all sprang from a conviction which my irresolution nearly killed at birth!

Frederick Coutts, *My Call to the Ministry*

Don't allow the world's praise to attract, or its blame to affright you from the discharge of the duty you owe to God, to yourself, or to the souls of those about you. God will take care of your reputation if you make his glory and your own duty your sovereign aim.

William Booth, 18 May 1909

From a cutting found amongst the General's papers following his promotion to Glory.

Contents

CHAPTER ONE

No man's land

Though 'the war to end all wars' had been over for several months, on that mid-summer's day in 1919, in the heart of the West Riding of Yorkshire, a sense of relief was still in the air. It was almost tangible. This was a time to be happy and all that the crowds of people on Peep Green wanted to do was to dance and dance and dance. That in itself was not strange, but the playing of a waltz by the Batley Castle Band of The Salvation Army to which reunited wives and husbands, mothers and sons, sweethearts and children were dancing, that was out of the ordinary. What had begun as an open-air service to thank God that a war which, in the words of one commentator, had made Europe 'a bankrupt slaughterhouse', was over, had become another kind of celebration.

The bandmaster, Will Spencer, on leave from the Forces at the time, smiled to himself as he thought about what was happening. Earlier in the day, with his twenty-five bandsmen and entourage, he had travelled on the open-top tram from Batley to the Hightown terminus from where it was still a good walk across the fields to Hartshead and Peep Green. There, out in the wilds, with a majestic view over Yorkshire moorland, the band should have provided music for a peace celebration service only—not for dancing.

Peep Green had seen greater crowds: 250,000 people had gathered there for a Chartist rally nearly eighty years previously. Furtively, Luddites had crossed her paths on their way to secret meeting places to plan the destruction of the machinery threatening their livelihood. There was always great excitement as miners and mill workers roared 'their bets' on to win at the horse-racing there. But never

1

before had Peep Green been host to such pure delight and genuine happiness. The war was well and truly over. It seemed the dancing would never end.

The small mining village of Hartshead had been badly affected by the war: twenty-four of her men had died; but those who had assembled for the service had travelled for many miles around to be present. It wasn't just a village affair. This was a day for a man's best clothes, his brightly coloured neckerchief and his highly polished Sunday clogs with glinting brass studs and toe-caps.

Occasionally the sunlight would catch a row of new, proudly worn medals, or a silver watch chain hanging across the waistcoat of a more prosperous—or thrifty—Yorkshireman.

Some of the women with their long dark woollen shawls around their shoulders, leaned against the high, dry stonewalls chatting. Even though their high-buttoned shoes tapped to the music, their concern was for the rationing, the spate of recent strikes and the shortage of money. Times were hard. It seemed that everyone had lost somebody in the 1,500 days of killing. The talk was of men returning blinded, crippled or shell-shocked; those still missing and those who would never be coming back at all to the back-to-back terrace houses in which they had grown up. But the dancing carried on.

As soon as the service was over someone had asked the Salvation Army bandmaster if he had a tune to which the people could dance, and so the melody of the old gospel song 'Calvary's stream is flowing' was chosen. The people started to dance and if they were tired of the one and only three-quarter-time tune which the salvationists were playing, they didn't show it. In fact they kept asking for more. The best traditions of puritan, chapel-going religion could, for just this once, be broken.

Bandmaster Spencer looked across at the latest addition to his band, a tall, thin young man not yet twenty years of age, recently demobbed from the Royal Flying Corps. 'He's a grand euphonium player,' thought Will Spencer to himself, 'but he hardly says a word.'

Relieved to be back in civvy street, Frederick Coutts, the newcomer, was definitely no extrovert, but the occasion appealed enormously to his razor-sharp sense of humour. His new friends, John Lowe demobbed a few months before, John Laxton, and Hanley Redfearn were not going to forget the occasion quickly either. The four had become good friends in the short time since Frederick had arrived in Batley to rejoin his Salvation Army officer parents Commandant and Mrs John Coutts.

Frederick's family was used to moving and since he had joined the Forces had come to live in the heart of the heavy woollen district. This was the land of 'mungo' and 'shoddy'; ham teas and co-operative societies; and the 'knocker-upper', a man who, summer and winter, at half past five in the morning tapped on bedroom windows with a long stick to wake those who had to go to work.

There was cold tea in a billy-can and sometimes only dripping on a man's bread for his 'snap' if he worked down the mine or in the mill. The hours were long, the pay was low, and conditions were poor. Leisure was found at the chapel or the working men's clubs.

The soot and smoke from the mill chimneys blackened the lungs of the Batley-ites and disfigured the proud yellow Yorkshire-stone-built churches and chapels, town hall and library. Life was as hard as the large cobble-stones on Batley market-place.

Commandant and Mrs John Coutts had arrived in the town on 15 May 1919. The health of their younger son, Ernest, four years junior to Frederick, was already giving rise to some concern. So much so that several young boys from the corps would go and stay with Ernest in the quarters whilst his parents were at the hall.

The commandant, an intelligent man and gifted speaker was a Scot, 'reserved and sparing of speech, at times as silent as the mountain lochs in his own country'. Before reaching the age of thirteen he had run away from his village home just outside Aberdeen to find work in Dundee. Returning to Aberdeen some time later, he met up with The Salvation Army, was converted and eventually applied to become an officer. His family were so unhappy about his plans that they wrote to the Army authorities saying he was dying of consumption and to William Booth saying that the youth was out of his mind.

On 1 March 1888 Cadet-Captain Coutts was appointed to Stotfold after just ten weeks training. However in 1919, thirty years on, the commandant was, as they say in Yorkshire 'a poorly man'. Sunday meetings took their toll of his strength and as soon as the evening meeting was over, exhausted, he made his way home and went directly to bed.

Frederick's mother, christened Mary Jones, had been brought up in the Welsh hills of Merioneth and 'had a share of that Celtic temperament which must find emotional expression'. Commissioned a Salvation Army officer in June 1891 and appointed back to Wales, she spent several years working in country districts and remote villages where Welsh, her first language, was also the language of the people. Until her dying day she said her private prayers and read her Bible in Welsh.

Her officership was full of self-sacrifice, devoted to the needs of others, and no task was beneath her. Mary Jones married Ensign John Coutts in October 1898 in Perth. Frederick was born at 2.15 pm on 21 September the following year in West Gallatown, in the Royal Burgh of Kirkcaldy, on the northern shores of the Firth of Forth. This Scottish birthright was something he would use to maximum advantage throughout his life.

In those days permanency played no part in the life of Salvation Army officers. When Frederick was just eight weeks old, his parents were on the move to Penicuik. His life was to be full of such changes: packing, cleaning, saying farewell, travelling, being welcomed, unpacking and settling-in. On 22 August 1903, at Yeovil, his brother Ernest was born.

Move followed move: Barnstaple, Cardiff, Bristol, Street, Loughborough, St Helens, Warrington, and back to Scotland. Frederick had attended eleven different schools in just ten years. In 1908 his classroom seat was 'a place at a long continuous desk, which stretched the

4

width of the classroom', in which he was provided with a slate and a slate pencil. He later wrote: 'My mortification arose from the fact that the class into which I was placed was already doing "pounds, shillings and pence". This stage in my formal education had not been reached at the country school from which I had come.' That morning a very disconsolate nine-year-old boy made his way home for dinner. He had not been able to get one sum right.

At another stage in his education, when his father was ill, the family went to stay in Barmouth on the Welsh coast where, though the lessons were in English, he also had to struggle with the ancient Cymric tongue. At Warrington he and Ernest were able to attend the same school with the grand sounding name of the People's College, for which privilege the boys' parents had to pay several pence per child, per week.

Even though he was a keen reader, there was not even a library at one of his Scottish secondary schools. No one guided his reading and consequently it became too discursive. Even Shakespeare was not popular north of the border. At Leith Academy there was neither sport nor music on the curriculum. Apart from woodwork there was nothing of a lighter nature. Only English, maths, art, a foreign language, science, geography and history. But there his intelligence was recognised, one teacher asking him if he had ever considered going to university. He would have liked to have gone but was so uninformed about the world in general that apart from this being some kind of dream city for him, it was an unattainable goal: in those days you had to have money to go to university. But he saw no reason to shed tears about it then and made his peace with the matter, nor did he later feel cheated by not having that higher education.

In all those changes of home and school the vital art of survival, essential to Salvation Army officers' children if they are to lead a happy life, had to be learned. 'Columbus was not more elated on sighting the new world than we were to explore the new quarters where we were to live. Would there be two single beds in our bedroom, or was it—as usual—one double bed between us? . . . Nevertheless upstairs, downstairs, in my lady's chamber we wandered, eager to discover any new delights—if thus they could be described,' he wrote later. 'Each move brought more than another corps to be sampled and another town to be explored . . . new schools, new masters, new standards, new lessons, new punishments, new playmates, new slang and new laws—almost entirely unwritten—as to what was and was not permissible. Let no one imagine that because that human animal, the small boy, is superficially the same all over Great Britain . . . the same yardstick can everywhere be applied. For one thing, his loyalties vary. The Merseyside lad's pride in his twin First Division football teams is not shared in Portsmouth. . . . The Glasgow urchin's joy in a trip "doon the watter" is unknown to the youth of the Midlands.'

'Again, the existence and use of boyish passwords varies from place to place. This is more than a variation in dialect, which is picked up unconsciously and dropped almost as rapidly, especially if the stay in any one district be short.' This all served to sharpen the boys' wits. It taught them that 'there was more than one parish pump in Great Britain. The world did not begin and end with any one town or country.'

But if all this sounds romantic, an echo from an unspoiled innocent bygone childhood, longing to be recaptured, it would be false. There were 'one or two horrid' moments for the two boys, especially in the places where The Salvation Army wasn't too popular. The violence may have been only verbal but for these two sensitive spirits it was hard to bear. 'One result of this continued changing was that Ernest's friendships were never of that intimate quality which come from a slow, steady growth over the years. The lad never had a boon companion with whom he could discuss any mortal subject under the sun', Coutts reflected on his brother's life, but was it not also some kind of reflection upon his own reservedness?

'This kind of wandering life might have been expected to turn out a pair of crazy, mixed-up kids,' he wrote, 'but amid all these changes and chances there was one constant factor—The Salvation Army. Faces, accents and streets might vary . . . but wherever we went there was always a Salvation Army corps with its attendant activities which never palled and of which there were never too many. Meetings, music and marchings were our life. At that age we neither asked nor wanted more.'

The boys' world was indeed the Army, they spent their leisure time at the Army: it was a punishment not being allowed to attend. The fun of learning to play a brass instrument, the fulfilment it gave the two boys and their pleasure at listening to the better bands was immeasurable. They were confirmed brass band fanatics.

When it came to the annual self-denial week, life was even more austere than usual. 'There was an ascetic note in the air. . . . Life was real and life was earnest. Certain goodies were conspicuous by their absence. Sweets were untasted for eight days: two Sundays counted at each end of the week. The breakfast porridge was unsweetened, cake disappeared from the tea-table, and the proceeds of this personal and compulsory denial' were to be seen in the brothers' altar service envelopes.

On Wednesdays the literature parcel arrived from the Army's printing house in time for the sale of the papers on the following Friday or Saturday. But the papers had to be folded before being passed over to the salvationists who sold them in the public houses. The machines which print, fold, count and deliver in one operation were not yet in use and so printer's ink covered the boy's hands before they finished that particular weekly chore.

The enemy of this way of life was 'the world', an omnibus phrase that covered a society that was full of hidden dangers for the unsuspecting salvationist boy or girl. 'My parents, from the highest of motives and with my concern genuinely at heart, wanted to shield me from "the world". I see now that this was an impossible task. It would have been dreadful if I had been born into some kind of home where they didn't care what their family did, or how they behaved and for me the Army world was a wonderful world.'

7

And so he sang lustily:

I'm at home in the Army more than I am anywhere,
You can dress as you like, you can sit where you like,
You're all quite equal there.
They sing the kind of songs I love,
*   so merry, bright and free,*
I'd have you to know, wherever I go,
The Army's the place for me.

The Army was never run down in the home and neither was there ever any 'Army gossip'. There was never criticism of the Army's leaders nor any discussion of local corps problems in front of the boys who were brought up in total ignorance of all these matters.

Frederick's parents were hard working, totally devoted corps officers with a social conscience. There was a miners' strike whilst they were stationed at Warrington and Mrs Coutts was immediately involved in providing the needy families with food parcels. Frederick's father would regularly walk the five miles to Winwick to visit one of the elderly soldiers and deliver the Army's papers. Though there was no money to pay for any form of transport the people had to be visited.

One of the most formative influences upon Frederick's life occurred when he was not yet thirteen years of age and William Booth visited his parents' corps at Warrington. The Founder had accepted the invitation of a rather wealthy man in the area who was favourable to the Army. It was 28 April 1912, and what was not realised at the time, was that this was to be the Founder's last Sunday public ministry in an English corps. There was no television, no radio, no public address system and to see the great man in the flesh was an unforgettable experience for salvationists whatever their age. The Sunday afternoon and evening meetings were held in the Hippodrome, a local theatre with two spacious galleries. This was situated in the centre of town and was made available free of charge. 'Whether the stage was occupied by a stand-up comic or a preacher of the gospel he had to use his voice, and his listeners had to lend him their ears.'

The Founder was then eighty-three years old, partially blind, and had been a widower for more than twenty years. Following his afternoon lecture word began to circulate that the General was not well and might be too ill to be present at the salvation meeting. However his cab eventually arrived. It was reported how weary the 'old warrior' was and that he apologised for being unwell and therefore not able to speak to them about their salvation 'with the forcefulness he desired. But a few moments later the miracle we had so often seen was repeated. The vigour of youth returned to the voice of the speaker, and with back unbent and words that rang clear and strong throughout the building, he forced upon the attention of those to whom he was speaking the importance of choosing to serve Christ. . . . Before the overmastering passion for the salvation of souls which possessed him . . . weariness and weakness were forgotten.'

Young Frederick was captivated whilst the General spoke about Pilate's question regarding Jesus: 'What shall I do then with Jesus which is called Christ?' And even though Frederick had been brought up to believe that the Founder was little less than an angel, to that schoolboy the half-blind General represented a lonely figure seated in his chair on the stage. 'Three or four women officers in the ungainly bonnets and voluminous dresses of those late Edwardian days made their way on to the stage to bend over his hand and kiss it. . . .' 'Their spontaneous action was not just a token of their affection; it was a sign of their reverence.'

Two weeks later the family moved again, but Frederick was never to forget this tableau and perhaps it was this scene in the final months of the Founder's life which kindled a flame of passionate interest in his mind for Salvation Army history.

Frederick's mother possessed a strong personality and dominated the family. Her will was of iron and her word was law. Everything in the home she made was just-so; she knew how to cook and bake well. If she thought the visitor needed only two slices of bread, then they received only two slices. Money was scarce and could not be wasted, but Frederick was going to learn to play the piano. His mother was determined he should. At first all they had was a small portable organ which could be folded up into a large rectangular box. Lessons were expensive: one shilling per hour and a shilling was 'a coin of destiny' for them: a married officer's salary with two children was little more than thirty shillings a week.

Neither was it the age of clever, pleasant or easy tunes for beginners: Frederick slaved over scales and Czerny's five-finger exercises. And neither was it music all the way: the necessary parental pressure had to be applied in order to make him practise. Coutts said that his teacher had placed a key in his hand which was to open a door upon a world he was still exploring seventy years later. When a second-hand piano was purchased for fifteen pounds, a fortune had been spent. Every time the family moved, packing the piano in its case and protecting it with pillows and blankets took on a solemn ritual.

Outside their home, poverty was everywhere and the two boys were to observe it first-hand, especially when their parents were stationed at Leith, just before the outbreak of the First World War. During the winters of 1912 and 1913, Mrs Coutts would go and help the other salvationist women who, five times a week, had been up since before dawn preparing farthing breakfasts. These consisted of oatmeal porridge which was cooked in an outsize copper in the ground floor kitchen of the Army hall. Soon after seven o'clock 300 children queued outside in the cold with their enamel bowls and spoons in their hands. Most were without shoes; all were without adequate food.

After climbing out of their hole-in-the-wall bed, Frederick and Ernest would first wash and then eat their own breakfast of porridge before scuttering across to the young people's hall to watch the tail-end of the queue of children being served. For him it was 'an early lesson in human need. The hungry must be fed'. These childhood memories and his later experiences as a corps officer in the 1930s probably confirmed him in his personal convictions concerning socialism.

If life was hard for the working classes, it was not much better for Salvation Army officers. Coutts knew what it was to be poor; poverty was on his parents' doorstep, too. Writing about those times he comments: 'Should any student of religious affairs wish to enquire how the work of The Salvation Army in Great Britain was steadfastly maintained until upborne on a wave of public popularity evoked by public service during two world wars, he should not overlook the uncomplaining willingness of many officers to live on a shoestring for the sake of the cause.'

Though his parents made their uncomplaining way around the country the years of corps officer commitment had begun to take its toll on Frederick's father. In addition to the strain of the work, 'there was little uplift in the constant struggle to keep body and soul together'. When stationed at St Helens in 1909, the commandant had been obliged to take time off because of illness and a few years later in Scotland he became ill once more.

'Worry and weakness laid him low; for weeks the household moved about on tiptoe. A prey to overstrained imagination, the sick man would feel himself losing grip and demand that the doctor be called at once; unless that were done, he would never see the night through. "One of the lads can go," would be the cry. Well, the boys knew it was no use; the doctor wouldn't come; there was nothing he could do, anyway. But to soothe his father, Ernest would slip out now and again into the darkness . . . and walk around for twenty minutes. By that time his father, comforted by the impression that the doctor was being sent for, would have fallen into an uneasy sleep.' This was a strange irony for, hanging in their home, almost mockingly, were the words of Deuteronomy 33:25 'As thy days, so shall thy strength be.'

Except for his great shyness Frederick was a boy like all other boys, and those crucial adolescent years were full of boyish things. Whilst living at Leith he was fascinated by the electric and cable trams, by the trains and their time-tables. He knew the stations, the routes and the fares. He studied and memorised them as only a small boy could. And about that time another important

11

event occurred in his life which was to awaken him to another world—the world of the Spirit.

'I prefer to see myself as a young teenager, with few interests beyond *The Gem* and *The Magnet* and a nominal supporter of a football team which, in the stern discipline of First World War days, I never saw play, fidgetting on the hard Presbyterian seat of the church in the Scottish village where my parents were holidaying. All the same, I was not to forget that Sunday evening. . . . Of a sudden my fidgetting ceased for, from the Old Testament lesson there fell on my ears several Bible phrases which I had never heard before or, if I had, I had not taken any notice of them—''Or ever the silver cord be loosed, or the golden bowl be broken, or the pitcher be broken at the fountain, or the wheel broken at the cistern.'' I had no clear idea what the words meant. I certainly did not know this was Ecclesiastes 12:6. But in those short phrases was a grave beauty, a sombre majesty I had not known before. Having ears, for the first time, I was hearing.'

But if his personal world was undergoing changes of emphasis and interest, the world in general was about to experience a war of such horrific proportions that life would never be the same again for millions of people.

In the years prior to the First World War there was no compulsory military service in Great Britain and even after war was declared in 1914 the government remained firmly against introducing it, believing that a volunteer force was better motivated and more deeply committed to fighting an enemy than any number of pressed men. Therefore, despite his forecast that millions of recruits would be needed for a combat lasting three or four years, Lord Kitchener, the Secretary of State for War, had to rely on men taking the 'King's shilling'. A great nation-wide recruiting campaign was launched to whip up emotions and patriotism in the hearts of young men and make them want to go to war. Posters appeared everywhere.

'Another call. More men and still more until the enemy is crushed', cried Lord Kitchener from one such poster. 'Remember Belgium', pleaded another. The friendly approach was not missed either: 'Come along, boys! Enlist today'—invited a relaxed, happy pipe-smoking soldier. Aimed at the more thoughtful was the stark picture of a soldier crossing a battlefield and the text: 'THINK! Are you content for him to fight for YOU? Won't you do your bit? We shall win but YOU must help. JOIN TODAY.'

But at the height of the war it became necessary to conscript and whatever the reason, and in answer to whatever argument, it was in the summer of 1917, when Frederick was just three months short of his eighteenth birthday, that he stood in a recruiting office, in Bath Street, Glasgow, near to the office in which he worked, to sign up to fight for king and country. His father was not convinced about this move. His mother prayed for him.

When calling up papers required him to present himself at the same office, a kindly sergeant suggested that he present himself at another table where applications for commissions were handled. This, he later interpreted, as the sergeant judging him 'unable to stand the rigours of a private of the line and, having inquired about his schooling, commended him to God and the Royal Flying Corps'.

It was every man for himself in the services. This style of life was rather different from his sheltered Salvation Army existence, however satisfying that might have been. There were sergeant-majors for whom swearing was their mother tongue. Many other aspects of service life were equally distasteful for him and so he kept a low profile while the rough corners were knocked off.

When he joined up in November 1917, his pay was a shilling a day out of which he made an allowance to his mother of sixpence a day. This was deducted from his salary. His father being ill, she needed the money badly. When he went for his first pay packet and stood at the table, cap off, at attention, waiting to salute, it was to salute for three and sixpence. 'I couldn't paint the old town red on three and sixpence: I needed it to buy cups of tea and buns.'

The official service record of Second Lieutenant

Frederick Coutts 45820 is as sparse as his own willingness to speak about his service career. For the most part he only ever talked about those eighteen months of military service with tongue in cheek. He even convinced one listener that to test the strength and direction of the wind whilst flying, they hung a piece of string over the side of the aircraft.

Following his posting to Farnborough, he first flew from Eastchurch aerodrome on the island of Sheppey. Flying was primitive. The biplane propellor was swung to start the machine and the flyers wore their ordinary uniforms with the only added comfort of goggles and a helmet. There was little protection against the weather. The pilot sat in the front seat and the observer sat directly behind him at the rear—and they didn't even bother to strap themselves in. Two homing pigeons were taken along to carry messages back in case of emergency.

If the plane reached 1,500 feet they were doing well. To facilitate radio contact in morse code, the wireless aerial, a cable on a drum in the fuselage, could be released only after the plane had reached a height of 250 feet, and had to be wound in before landing. This was part of eighteen-year-old Frederick's responsibility.

Second Lieutenant Coutts flew as an observer. And even though mounted before him was a machine gun, beneath him bombs ready to be dropped, and fixed to his waist a pistol, he never fired a shot in anger, caused any damage, shot anyone down, nor was he ever the victim of any warfare. The British War medal, the only medal he was entitled to, according to his service record, was never even issued to him. It was an uneventful time: there were no thrilling adventures to be savoured and told to his grandchildren.

In September 1918 Frederick was posted to the Aegean Group. There was talk of a second offensive with air support and so along with several other young airmen he was posted to Mudros in the Eastern Mediterranean, to an airfield which was within striking distance of the Dardanelles. But his long journey by train and boat was not really necessary. The offensive was never launched and peace quickly returned to the region. Family tradition has it that he also flew over parts of Turkey trailing white peace ribbons because of some problems there with the cease fire. However, within a few weeks he was on his way home again.

The Great War for civilisation was over by the winter of 1918. The problem of demobilising so many men with all the attendant problems of unemployment, was begun. Whilst waiting to become a civilian again, Coutts was posted to a seaplane station in Scotland where, for weeks on end, no religious services were held and there was no chaplain to be seen. The nearest church was several miles away and he became aware of the fact that unconsciously he was beginning to lose a sense of what personal knowledge he had of 'Christ as a present Companion'.

Knowing something had to be done about this matter he made the corps at Aberdeen Citadel his spiritual home and in his free time was able to visit friends of his parents, the divisional chancellor, Brigadier and Mrs Alleine Sewell. On one occasion Mrs Sewell was about to hang up some recently washed curtains when Frederick arrived. She asked if he would mind hanging them for her and couldn't understand his hesitancy. What she didn't know was that he had just been involved in a forced landing and wasn't yet fully over the shock. It was only with great difficulty that he dared stand on a chair to hang the curtains. Apart from such near misses life on the base was boring.

There was literally nothing for him to do at his last posting, Strathbeg. From January until April his only task was to listen for the twelve o'clock time signal on the radio and then telephone the adjutant's office and the officers' mess with the time check. With that his day's work was completed.

On 16 April 1919 Coutts was posted to a dispersal centre, glad to be released from 'a way of life largely at variance' with everything he had been taught or had known. His reflections upon those war years were crystal clear:

War and post-war were two sides of the same traumatic

experience. The carefree climate of a flying station was no preparation for a return to the sobrieties of civilian life. If to eat of the tree of knowledge of good and evil meant the end of domestic innocence, the chill realities of the post-war labour market soon exposed the hollowness of the stock judgments of the officers' mess. This was the old 'one-two'—the first blow which stood you up for the second to lay you flat on your face. Only this was not taken on the point of the chin but on the more sensitive areas of heart and mind.

No one had explained 'with what little wisdom the world is governed'. 'Nor had I,' he wrote later, 'yet perceived that the heaviest casualties in any war are sustained by the work of God, and that an international movement such as The Salvation Army is more vulnerable than most. I was a late developer!'

But where was he to go? He was not yet twenty years old. As always, his home was where his parents were and that, in the spring of 1919, was Batley in the West Riding of Yorkshire.

CHAPTER TWO

The breath of a light whisper

In 1919 Europe was preoccupied with the consequences of the Great War. How could it be otherwise? Every city and village was busily planning and financing ways to honour their dead. News was continually arriving of missing soldiers being confirmed dead. Prisoners of war were being repatriated. Other families were left only to brood over the uncertain fate of their loved ones. Those who had returned were not experiencing a land fit for heroes either.

Coutts had no plans for the future. He had been fortunate enough to find work in Leeds in the offices of Montague Burton, 'the nation's tailors'. A friendship with a young salvationist, Katie Roberts, who worked in the local library had come to nothing. With his friends he attended the local band contests and concerts, but so far life for him had not been anything to shout about.

During those war years everything which he had loved, known and taken for granted had been challenged by, and exposed to, a completely different world with another set of standards. He enjoyed his Salvation Army banding but his taking his place in Batley Castle Corps was not due to any conviction or conscious decision: the Army was his home and an intense loyalty to the movement which had offered him so much security in the past, governed his actions now. Besides, he had no other home to go to. He was in a state of limbo. What was he going to do with his life?

If military service had done nothing else for him, it had sharpened his mental hunger and he began to read everything on which he could lay his hands. What he could not buy he could borrow was his maxim, besides there

17

was plenty of time to read on his daily tram journey to work. Whilst he looked through the rows of books in the Carnegie Library on Batley market-place, the Westminster chimes of the clock vibrated throughout the whole building. But again the reading was a hit and miss affair: 'I embarked on my private explorations without knowing how to explore, nor even the name of the country I was seeking. I read at random, haphazardly, voraciously, doubtless unwisely, hardly understanding what I was reading much less what I should read—for because of my inbuilt reserve I hesitated to ask any man to guide me.'

But if there was no one leading him to the right books, the Holy Spirit was leading him towards the revealed will of God. The state of limbo was soon to pass. Yet, right to the end of his days, he always took great pains to emphasise that that revelation had never been a Damascus Road experience; that for him there had never been any brightly flashing spiritual lights. It was much more subtle and sensitive than that, and besides, anything more dramatic would have only embarrassed him and made him even more reluctant to believe what was happening to him.

There are two recorded occasions on which he was aware of the growing notion to become a Salvation Army officer. One was on a Sunday evening, whilst sat in his customary place at the huge and ancient American organ which provided music in the Batley Castle hall, a building comfortably seating 1,500 people. As usual, his father was leading the meeting: 'I was given no vision, I heard no voice speaking in the English tongue. No bright light from Heaven shone round about me. It came home to me . . . that the proclamation of the salvation of God in Christ Jesus should be my vocation. I sat on the organ stool outwardly unchanged. Of what had happened I told no man, not even my parents, but made my private application to the appropriate Salvation Army authority. And no sooner had made it but wished to withdraw it. . . . Any conviction was at first no larger than a grain of mustard seed but this has since grown to such a size as to dominate my life.' His life was set on a new course and everything he subsequently said and did was related to that moment.

The second occasion was as follows: 'Standing between the bookshelves of that library in the fading light of a summer evening, it occurred to me that the answer to my confusions might be to take the words of Jesus at their face value. He might even be right and these current counsellors wrong. I have written: "It occurred to me". A more confident spirit would have said: "The conviction took hold of me". But I must not falsify the record by ascribing to an uncertain lad the assurance which he did not possess.'

This decision to become a Salvation Army officer was 'a reversal of an adolescent attitude': he had shown absolutely no desire or capacity for public work. He was intensely shy. In the Sunday afternoon praise meeting brevity was the hallmark of his testifying: 'Saved and happy' was his customary announcement 'and if in some unexpected outburst of eloquence I elaborated on that bald statement adding "and on my way to Glory" that was a speech which absolved me from further public utterance for the rest of the week.'

One of the most humiliating experiences of his teenage years happened when he was invited by a kind-hearted divisional commander to 'special' at a nearby corps. In the evening meeting he was asked to speak, but even though he stood to his feet, he was unable to utter a single word. After a long silence he took his seat again. Here was no ambitious actor seeking centre stage and loud applause via the ministry. This overwhelming reservedness would follow him throughout his officership and continue to make difficulties for him, right to the end of his life. He was never to upstage anyone, or draw the spotlight away from his Saviour, the Army or anyone else—whoever it might be—so that the light would shine the more brightly upon himself.

But his decision was made. He signed the large blue candidates forms. Hesitantly he had chosen, but he did not allow the ordinariness of the experience to detract from its decisiveness. He went into officership with both eyes open, knowing he would have to live and work in the public eye despite his natural instinct to withdraw from such attention. There is no record of Cadet Frederick Coutts farewelling from Batley for London. The corps history book is strangely silent about its most illustrious son. Due to a nationwide train strike Coutts entered the gates of the Training Garrison in Linscott Road, London E5, on 7 October 1919, a few days later than the other 400 cadets of the Jubilee Session. It was a time of exciting expansion in the Army world.

Coutts once likened the training garrison experience to the service life he had left only five months before; much the same, only without the swearing. You took your orders and did as you were told: it was a strict regime. The 100 men cadets shared open dormitories in three Victorian houses in the Lower Clapton Road which they also kept clean under the watchful eye of the cadet-sergeants. Every morning before breakfast they marched to the garrison, and after supper marched back again. Three times a week the cadets attended their various training corps: for Cadet Coutts this was, until Christmas, Poplar Corps and afterwards the corps at Walthamstow. The cadets marched there and back every time.

There was neither sport nor any recreational activity. Improvisation had been the hallmark of service life and when a cadet discovered a discarded milk churn, another found a bat and a third a ball. The lads prepared for a game of cricket during the dinner hour in the large cemented yard behind the Congress Hall. This pleasure came to an abrupt end despite appealing to Scripture: 1 Timothy 4:8. Sport was not allowed. Half a day off per week was the only free time. The compulsory half-an-hour of private prayer was experienced in curtained-off cubicles. During that time, according to a report in *The War Cry*, the cadets were 'shaping themselves for a soul-saving career and wrestled secretly with God'.

Coutts' customary pose when sitting in a chair was to drape his long angular frame over the arms, back and seat, a lesson in relaxation which did not go down well with one training college officer who remarked: 'Coutts you sit in that chair like a rag doll!' He took his place in the cadets' band playing trombone, and if the record of his service in the Royal Flying Corps is sparse, any record of his time in training is even more obscure.

Let no one imagine that spending time in a Salvation Army training college changes a person's basic character overnight—if at all. Cadet Coutts was soon to be confronted with his essential character in an open-air meeting held one evening in a back street not far from the rear entrance to The Salvation Army's Mothers' Hospital. The new cadet was invited to give his own 'glowing, red hot, up-to-date personal experience'. But the leader also announced that he couldn't give Cadet Coutts too much time. But Coutts didn't want any time: he had never spoken in an open-air meeting in his life before.

He came face to face with some of The Salvation Army's living legends in the garrison, seeing and hearing such charismatic figures as John Lawley, Elijah Cadman, Mildred Duff, Frederick St George de Lautour Booth-Tucker, Samuel Brengle and also General Bramwell Booth 'towering' above them all. His chief side officer was Lieut-Colonel Alfred G. Cunningham, a man who would later play an important role in Frederick's life.

By Monday 3 May 1920 Frederick Coutts had become a probationary lieutenant. His formal training completed, he 'was not the young man in the flying machine who had entered Clapton eight months earlier. . . .' He was 'slowly unlearning the tawdry values acquired during the previous two years. It might not be inaccurate to describe this slow turn around as [his] "conversion". . . . The hardest part of [his] training was about to commence.'

Not yet twenty-one years of age, Coutts made his way to Blackpool Citadel where he was to become the second officer. For a young man who didn't naturally take to public work this was decisive for, apart from the normal corps programme, weather, wind and waves permitting, the corps held three meetings a day, five days a week on the famous seaside beach during the summer. Such was the pressure upon him that he learnt the discipline of

21

preparing as carefully for his open-air work as for any indoor meeting: 'These are the real life situations which test a man's ability to give a reason for the hope that is in him. They provide a severer ordeal than facing a captive audience in a university hall or a television studio. Such a company are prisoners for a set period. An open-air crowd can melt away in seconds as some of us have learnt to our cost.' His aim was to 'explain the truths of the Christian faith to non-churchgoing hearers in non-religious language—the simpler the better.' . . . In proclaiming the gospel the receiving end is all-important. What matters is not what I say but what my hearers understand me to say'.

However, it was not all hard: it was 'a wonderful appointment for a carefree lad'. It meant he had a home, with an officer and his wife who themselves had very young children. It meant he had a good corps with a congregation running to hundreds and the officer gave him the chance to preach often and regularly. It was in Blackpool that he first had the opportunity to preach from the pulpit of a church other than The Salvation Army: namely the Methodist Central Hall.

Frederick Coutts knew that if he was going to be a good officer he must learn to stand in other men's shoes and again he was a prisoner of his own nature. 'Here temperament was a handicap. Neither life in the Forces nor life in the training college had turned me into an extrovert. I was still reluctant to butt in on anyone else's affairs and could not bring myself to frame so blunt a question as: "Are you saved?" Intimate enquiries of that nature seemed to call for a more oblique approach. I did not rejoice in these inhibitions; how to be delivered from them was my problem.'

Within a few weeks of Frederick leaving for the training garrison in 1919, his parents were again on the move. Things went well for a time; Ernest found his musical feet and grew in stature as a pianist but Commandant Coutts became ill again and a complete rest was needed. Just three miles outside Warrington was the hamlet of Fearnhead where in one of the two streets were half a dozen semi-detached houses given to the Army for use of officers on sick furlough. Commandant and Mrs Coutts and Ernest made their way there. Warrington was not unknown to the Couttses. They had been stationed there ten years previously. What was now urgent was a source of income; even though Mrs Coutts was extremely thrifty, an officer's sick-pay was not sufficient to support all three of them. It fell to Ernest, now in his late teens, to provide for the family.

Of course Frederick visited his parents in Warrington and something he saw there in 1920 he never forgot. 'As the prayer meeting began, the assistant young people's sergeant-major—still a university undergraduate—rose from her place in the songsters and quietly moved to speak to one or two young people in the congregation to help them to a decision. What was done, and the way it was done, has never been forgotten by at least one who was there.'

This young songster was Bessie Lee. Attractive, intelligent and possessing a mind of her own, she would have made an impression upon any young man. Her beautiful singing voice had a charm all of its own. She and Frederick were of the same age and had also attended the People's College in Frogall Lane as children. They were not total strangers.

Bessie's father, Bandmaster James Lee, was a huge, barrel-chested man who was not only the foreman in the boiler-making yard at a large local iron works, Pearson and Knowles, but to all intents and purposes *was* The Salvation Army in Warrington: everyone in the town knew him. One visitor enquiring from a local policeman the address of the corps officer received as an answer: 'I don't know where he lives, but he works at Bewsey Forge.' But this is hardly surprising as he was bandmaster for more than forty years.

Bandmaster Lee was a good salvationist and knew that the Army world did not start nor end at Warrington. He was a good friend of Chalk Farm Band's legendary Bandmaster A. W. Punchard. When Chalk Farm Band bought saxophones, Warrington had to have them. When the London band bought trumpets, Lee had to purchase some for his men, too.

A number of the bandsmen worked under Lee's supervision at the iron works, but the corps was never mentioned at work and work was never mentioned at the corps. He was very strict about that. No one argued with James Lee either at work or at the Army. He was a disciplinarian of the first order, who conducted the band practices in his uniform, and because of some trouble with his legs leaned on his bicycle whilst marching at the front of the band.

His authoritarian manner did not suit everyone: some felt he had too much sway over what took place in the corps. It was a fact that the overpowering personality of the man overshadowed the other local officers and soldiers. Though he wasn't popular in some circles he was fair, generous and kind. Whenever there was an appeal for money he would recite:

> *There was a man,*
> *the people thought him mad,*
> *the more he gave away,*
> *the more he had.*

One of the first things Bandmaster Lee did when meeting new corps officers was to promise them that he would make sure that they regularly received their salary.

Bessie's mother was also a strong personality. A salvationist, she never wore uniform, but supported her husband in all he did. She was a good mother to their three children: Fred, a little on the serious side, and Harry and Bessie who loved a joke. There were three years between each of them. The family also owned a parrot which sang 'Glory for me'!

Though the Lee's were working class people they had an eye for their children's development and were not uninformed about higher education. On Mrs Lee's side various relatives had moved into the academic world. One had become a doctor, another had married a professor; in that sense it was also an unusual family for its day.

Bessie was a kind girl who grew up into a young woman

who had a way with people in general and a gift for communicating with teenagers in particular. Modesty was her hallmark: she dressed plainly in clothes made for her by her mother; there was never any show of any kind; everybody liked her. With her friend Margaret Siddle she cycled into the country on her regular rounds to sell the Army papers. Brilliant at school, she studied hard and passed her scholarship to the town's High School, eventually gaining a place at Manchester University where she studied science under 'the illustrious atomist', Lord Ernest Rutherford. Able to remain at home whilst studying, she travelled daily by train to Manchester. In the corps she was the life saving guard leader and assistant young people's sergant-major. At university she did not hide her soldiership under a bushel: on the white gown she wore in the laboratory was an Army brooch and during self-denial time she attended university in uniform so that she could go collecting afterwards. She never studied on a Sunday; Sundays were for the Army.

In an age when few salvationists obtained academic qualifications, when girls generally did not go to university and certainly not to study science, the bandmaster's daughter at Warrington earned herself a first class honours degree in chemistry, one of only two awarded that year. It is no wonder that she was the apple of her father's eye.

After qualifying, Bessie moved to London to teach at the John Howard Secondary School at Clapton, just two streets away from the training garrison and from where she could sometimes hear the sound of women cadets playing their tambourines. She taught chemistry but disliked the routine of teaching, feeling rather stifled in a tight roster and unable to be creative: she loved art. Despite the restrictions, the three-and-a-half years during which she was a teacher were her 'balmy days'. She took her place as a local officer in Wood Green Corps and later in Tottenham Citadel.

One Saturday morning about twelve months after arriving in Blackpool, Lieutenant Coutts opened a green-coloured envelope and read a letter which informed him that, with the rank of captain, he was being farewelled and was to take up his first corps as a commanding officer. He experienced a sinking feeling; no longer would he be able to refer his worries to the older and wiser man in whose house and family he had been so much at home. He was going to miss them. Neither was he to have a lieutenant and if he felt troubled on that Saturday morning he was forlorn on the Thursday afternoon when he said his goodbyes.

The corps, Blackburn IV, (Millhill) was there *en masse* to greet him at the station and march him to his new four-roomed home where they left him to eat a solitary tea and prepare his spirit for the welcome meeting that evening.

On most Friday mornings, before the mill buzzers had sounded, 'a young man, looking nervous and distrait, might have been seen stealthily swilling down his dozen yards of paving reaching from the front door to the front gate. Then, according to the good old Lancashire custom, the stone steps had to be whitened. . . .'

Inside life was simple. The front door opened into the living-room where a few square yards of linoleum called for a weekly polish. A large, black grate of pre-war design provided the heating and in the scullery there was 'a flagged floor innocent of any covering'. Upstairs the one-and-a-half rugs in the bedrooms needed to be shaken every week. This was a different world from Blackpool. In Blackburn he had a soldiers roll of fifty and an eight-piece band in which he had to play cornet—an instrument he never fully mastered.

Five months later, October 1921, came another change of appointment to the North-West divisional headquarters, in Preston, where he was to be the divisional helper—a sort of general, secretarial dog's-body—a post he held for three-and-a-half years. There he shared an office with the divisional chancellor, Brigadier Sewell, in whose house he had found a home whilst in the flying corps in Scotland. The two men shared an office 'in peaceful co-existence', only to be interrupted by the divisional commander wandering in to their office singing his theme song:

The mistakes of my life have been many,
The sins of my heart have been more,
And I scarce can see for weeping,
But I'll knock at the open door.

With the refrain:

I know I'm weak and sinful,
It comes to me more and more. . . .

'The mistakes of my life. . . .' This puzzled Coutts because he recalls, tongue in cheek, 'I had been brought up on the infallibility of Salvation Army leadership—at least from the office of divisional commander upwards. I think I know now what he felt his mistake had been, for he had been a provincial commander . . . had resigned, and had returned several rungs lower down. . . . None of us are infallible, not even the youngest of us.'

But Coutts was serious about resignation. When news came to him that one of his fellow cadets was about to resign, he was sorely troubled. He took a late train to a large provincial city paying his own fare and the cost of overnight lodgings out of his thirty shillings and sixpence salary so that first thing the next morning he could be on his way to knock on his friend's door and talk to him about his problems. Speed was of the essence. He felt that resignation was a betrayal of a divine vocation. He even called resignation 'defection'. This feeling never left him: 'I would call upon every officer to say: now is my soul troubled—over every defection, however few they may be. Were there only one I would call upon every officer to say: now is my soul troubled. That officer, or those officers, immediately charged with dealing with such a situation should be able not only to say: we are troubled but, on behalf of us all to say: every comrade officer is troubled . . . there ought daily to rise from us all a volume of corporate prayer for those who are tempted. Daily we should set a watch upon our lips lest some witty innuendo or brilliantly devastating half-truth seal the fate of someone whose steps have well nigh slipped.'

It was a theme he subsequently addressed as a Salvation Army leader, noticing that 'the suggestion to leave the path of duty often comes from a friend or relation. And when it comes from that source it is the harder to resist.' And then he would illustrate the commonness of this temptation with reference to General Albert Orsborn's temptation, when a young officer, to resign and emigrate to Canada where a church was waiting for him, and the young William Bramwell Booth who at the age of twenty-one in 1877 was 'much agitated' as to the future. He didn't think he could do the work and therefore 'a secular employment would certainly be much easier than this'. Coutts never chastised in those later sermons but pointed his hearers to Christ who himself withstood temptation and is able to succour those in difficulty.

During this divisional headquarters appointment Captain Coutts began to build up something of a reputation as a speaker. Regularly setting time aside to study, he was rarely seen without a book in his hand, never wasting a moment. He preached earnestly and unusually. What he said demanded attention because there was always an intelligent application to the Bible message he brought. At the same time people were noticing his peculiar mannerisms as he spoke in public. His nervousness whilst preaching caused him, for instance, continually to button and unbutton his tunic. Only those closest to him were aware of the tension and the personal cost of his public work. People also began to comment on the fact that, apart from his platform work, he didn't say much. He had no small talk, he was unable to commence simple conversation. People were often embarrassed and uncomfortable in his presence.

However, he was busy experimenting with other methods of communication and trying to inspire others to communicate the gospel more effectively. An article under his name was published in the November 1923 edition of *The Officer* magazine appealing for the salvationist to speak to the man in the street in a language he understands. 'We must become all things to all men, in order that we may capture some. To start with we may have to depict Jesus as a Great Adventurer instead of a Saviour. We may have to speak of Him as One who was a real sport; as One who never let a friend down. This can be done with reverence and without detracting from the divinity of His character.'

Music-making was still important to him and which brass band fanatic would refuse to play in his future father-in-law's band when asked? When Warrington Band auditioned at the Manchester BBC studios, Captain Fred Coutts helped out on bass and is seen holding a cornet on a later photograph of the band. On such occasions he could also visit his parents and see his brother again. Life in Warrington might have been happy so far as occasional music-making went, but matters took a shattering turn for the worse in February 1922 when a letter arrived from headquarters: Frederick's father, at the age of fifty-six, following thirty-four years of service as an officer, was to be retired. What was to be done? Where were they to go? How would they live? Frederick couldn't help; he had been an officer for just two years. Ernest was only eighteen years old. There was utter despair in the family.

Commandant Coutts wanted to return to Scotland. 'To Scotland! That meant another change. . . . Was there never to be any end to this nomadic existence? But his father, like a wounded creature dragging itself to its lair, wanted to end his days in the land of his birth. Uncomplainingly, Ernest followed.' Commandant and Mrs Coutts moved to a small flat in Glasgow and soldiered at the Parkhead Corps. For long enough Ernest couldn't find work, and when he did it wasn't much and didn't pay much either. There seemed little justice in life. Ernest was not settled.

During the next four years the commandant became increasingly ill, his 'gaunt face slowly tightening over his cheek and jaw bones'. Mrs Coutts was, for the most part, nursing him single-handed, day and night. His illness was protracted and incurable.

Three-and-a-half years after Frederick Coutts' arrival in Preston, another appointment came, as divisional helper to the Northern Division. It was February 1925. Bessie had entered the training college a few weeks before, much to the surprise and puzzlement of her teacher colleagues. They did not understand how she could now be trained by people who were academically inferior. Cadet Bessie Lee was not happy in the training garrison—unhappy enough for her fiancé to enter the fact in a short sentence in his diary. One of her teaching colleagues visited her one lunchtime and wrote: 'The drab interior of the building was repellant. The scrubbed floors had no carpet on them and when we were received by Bessie in her bare cubicle, we found her beautiful hands red with scrubbing for which she had to use carbolic soap.' Bessie's philosophy was that six months would pass quickly.

In Newcastle, Captain Coutts was still learning. One day he heard footsteps coming up to the first floor offices. It sounded like a man very much the worse for wear. 'He loudly announced that he needed help. My inexperienced judgment was that he needed a large cup of strong, hot, black coffee before he could profit by any help I might be able to give him. I was taking this line when he broke out with what sounded almost like a cry of despair. "Is there no one here then who will pray with me?" I had sufficient sense to forget the coffee and drop on my knees. I was slowly learning that this was the best way to get down to business.'

Captain Coutts' name appeared again in the September 1925 issue of *The Officer* under an article headlined 'Selflessness or Self-Interest'. Based on the text from John 3:30, 'He must increase, I must decrease', it was a plea for spiritual selflessness as the only solution to the problem of jealousy amongst equals:

> The true test of character comes when a man with whom we have walked side by side steps out and takes the prize upon which we had set our hearts. . . . The achievements of a great man arouse in us no envy, but rather admiration. The success of our neighbour, who is our equal, produces more mixed feelings within our breast. We question the worth of that success. . . . The naked truth is that most of us are constantly afraid that our neighbour will gain a march on us. We would like to follow the way of the Cross if everyone else did so. But we are certainly unwilling to count our ambitions

as dung and dross for Christ's sake, while others gain for themselves honour and favour among men. . . . Our Master must look in pity on those personal ambitions and petty vanities of ours which we hide so carefully from sight, yet cherish like the apple of our eye.

With Bessie first teaching in London and then entering the training garrison, and Coutts 'specialing' most weekends, there was little time for what most people would consider a normal courtship. But at least they could spend their holidays together. Mr and Mrs Lee, Frederick and Bessie, Harry and his girlfriend, Lena, went to the Isle of Man and wherever Coutts went there were always books. One day the four young people decided to go rowing; everyone was ready till Coutts came down the beach with some books under his arm. In no uncertain terms Harry reminded him that he was expected to row as well and need not bring any reading matter with him. But Coutts was a bad sailor and in a short time he was back in the hotel being violently sick.

Despite the fact that Bessie's mother was upset by her daughter's decision to become an officer, feeling that she had thrown away her academic achievements, and wasted her years of study, Bessie was commissioned an officer. The consequences of her academic training were going to make life even more difficult for her later in her officership. However in May 1925 she arrived at Hirst, her first corps appointment in the Northern Division, near to her fiancé. Hirst was a poor corps. The hall was a wooden hut, the soldiers considered a rag, tag and bobtail group.

On 14 November that same year Captain and Mrs Coutts were married in the Newcastle Temple Corps hall. Due to the commandant's illness, Coutts' parents could not be present at the wedding. No one will know the effect of Bessie's life and personality upon her husband, especially in the light of her academic achievements and his own brilliant but untrained mind and totally different temperament. Five days later the honeymoon couple took charge of their first corps together, at Chatham, one of the Medway towns, in Kent.

Because Ernest's prospects in Glasgow were so poor, he moved back to Warrington to find work. Commandant Coutts' condition deteriorated further: he became bedridden and grew daily weaker, but his 'ruling passion was strong even in death'. 'Whilst unconscious he imagined that he was conducting a meeting, and in appealing tones he warned sinners of the eternal truths concerning salvation. In his imagination there were men who came to the penitent form and finally he pronounced the benediction in a clear and distinct voice. He died as he had lived. His waking thoughts were wholly for the salvation of men, and in death he was not divided from them.'

CHAPTER THREE

Rightly handling the word of truth

Captain and Mrs Frederick Coutts became numbers 154 and 155 respectively on the soldiers' roll at Chatham where the demanding corps programme allowed them no time to honeymoon. There was a great deal of work to do in this busy seaport with its naval dockyard and garrison. Apart from a busy weekend schedule of Sunday-schools, indoor and outdoor meetings, there were also public meetings held every Monday, Wednesday, Friday and Saturday evening. This demanded a constant supply of new material because the band and songster brigade were regularly present and other soldiers must also hear something new and edifying. The captain was having to spend many hours in his study preparing Bible talks for these occasions; this was something quite different from anything he had yet experienced as an officer at Blackpool or on a divisional headquarters. 'My passionate interest is in men who do work which corresponds the closest to that of a corps officer of The Salvation Army, and who stick to that last all their days,' he wrote. 'I learn, not from the man who delivers one good address at one hundred different meetings, but from the man who delivers one hundred consecutive addresses of a consistent standard to the same congregation.'

At the same time Mrs Coutts was creating quite a reputation with her beautiful singing voice and was becoming popular as a speaker at women's meetings in the town.

On Saturday evenings the band, songster and corps cadet brigades would be on duty at the open-air meeting held on the corner of Batchelor Street; the many late night shoppers making an interested congregation for the salvationists. Because Chatham was full of sailors and soldiers many prostitutes were also working in the town, especially in the area known as 'The Brook'. There the cheap and filthy lodging houses made it a notoriously dangerous district for innocents abroad. Depravity and drunkenness were the norm. Mrs Captain Coutts and the corps cadet brigade were responsible for *The War Cry* ministry in the public houses during which no one ever dared enter a tavern alone: that was only asking for trouble.

On Sunday evenings the songster brigade would sing in the open-air meeting; the band, corps cadet brigade and young people's corps were in attendance and it was a sight to see the salvationists, colours flying, marching to the hall along the busy Chatham High Street. Sometimes on Sunday evenings, instead of attending the salvation meeting, the corps cadet brigade would visit the notorious lodging houses in 'The Brook', to try to reach the people with the good news of the gospel.

The corps was not without its problems. The elderly bass drummer who only ever played the instrument indoors, was past his prime. With so much open-air work, a drummer was badly needed who could play in the streets and on the march. But retirement was out of the question! And in protest one Sunday evening the drummer, complete with his family and the bass drum, beat a hasty and somewhat emotional retreat home. Captain Coutts was faced with reclaiming the drummer, the drum and the family.

He learnt another valuable lesson: 'My training in my calling continued. Some lessons were palatable; some were not; all were needful. I had to learn to keep my cool so that, whatever disagreements arose, I would never be on such bad terms with any of my people that I could not visit them in their homes or kneel with them in prayer. I repeat: this I had to learn—the hard way, for nothing does more damage to an officer's ministry than a breach which determines which homes he visits and which he does not.'

Within a few months of their arrival the young officer-bride became pregnant and needed some help in the large, strangely constructed quarters in Luton Road. Their one and only material treasure was a Bechstein upright piano which Bessie had brought with her. A young salvationist, Florrie Hales, volunteered to help. Twice a week she came: on Mondays because it was wash-day and on Fridays 'to clean through'.

Margaret Lee Coutts, their first daughter, was born on Christmas day 1926 in the Mothers' Hospital in Clapton. Florrie was allowed to do the honours of preparing the tea and making sure the coal fire was lit for mother and baby's home-coming. A short time later Mrs Commandant Coutts visited Chatham to dedicate her grandchild to God.

Whilst her parents were leading the meetings, Margaret was left in the officers' room at the back of the hall and someone would be posted to listen for her cries, but they were rarely heard. The proud father had his own method of preparing his daughter for the homeward journey. He would lay Margaret's silver grey shawl out on the table and roll her up in it instead of wrapping it round her.

Among those who greatly influenced Coutts and helped determine many of his attitudes was Lieut-Colonel Gustave Isely who visited the corps on 28 February 1926 to lead meetings. Isely was a Swiss, French-speaking officer who was essentially a teacher noted for his absolute integrity, simplicity, humility and love.

Isely hated all forms of pomp and attached little importance to rank or title, believing that the message was of supreme importance and the messenger none. He didn't like a fuss being made of him nor did he care for flattering introductions or presentations. He preferred to talk to soldiers and young officers rather than to the more important personages. In his own way he was a rebel, possessing a gentle humour. He disliked extravagance of any kind: 'The Army's money was God's money, the money of the poor,' and it had to be spent wisely, even to the detriment of his own health. He loved words and his literary contributions in French and English enriched the Army for many years. He delighted and excelled in being able to write articles and books of an instructional nature and which demanded thorough research. His pen was rarely idle. At one time ninety-eight of the 500 songs in the French song book were written by Gustave Isely.

Born in La Béroche, a farming community in the canton of Neuchâtel, in 1879, Isely possessed a refined character but his reserve often intimidated people and he was never completely free from 'this restraint'. However, behind the modesty there was a superior knowledge and judgment, but it was his godliness which was his most attractive quality. Possessing a slight cockney accent Isely had an easy, cultured style of oratory, remembering and gladly speaking about what he owed to the Army; to the salvationists who had guided and helped him. Though his life as an Army officer was hard on his basic disposition, he was one of the movement's intellectuals and 'an excellent recruiting sergeant for the Army'.

Amongst his appointments in Britain were those of assistant candidates' secretary and young men's counsellor in which capacity he helped hundreds of young men. Later, as a territorial commander, though he tried to be a brother to the younger officers he was not soft with them. As an Army leader, chief secretary and territorial commander, there was authority and power in his hand-written letters; he could discipline and rebuke where necessary. He could be so strict that he was thought too severe on occasions. It is not hard to see why Coutts was so attracted towards him as mentor and friend: they had so much in common. 'To listen to him was to have one's ears opened as to how the word of God should be explained and applied. To share his conversation over the meal table was to have a new vision of what it meant to sing "The world for God". To note how he led a congregation in worship . . . was to be taught what a Salvation Army meeting could be like. From him I never had a penny. What he gave me was without money and without price—the spiritual and mental stimulus of his fellowship.'

Alongside his corps work, Coutts was learning to communicate with thousands of people around the Army world through his writings. Whilst teaching in London,

Bessie had made friends with a young officer, Madge Unsworth, a member of the editorial department. They became close friends and perhaps that is why Frederick Coutts decided to send his first manuscripts to *The Warrior*, a magazine for young people on which Madge Unsworth worked.

His motives were pure enough. In a light-hearted article in *The Warrior* he later described how it all began. He had several boyhood friends who had begun to make their way in the world of journalism and it fired something in him:

> Contrary to my friends' ways, however, I was not out to make my fortune by writing. I wished to help the Movement in which I had been born and bred. That desire could not be repressed. The goodness that was in me persisted in breaking through. I therefore made my first offer to the lesser magazines, the monthlies . . . I was also prepared—and this but further illustrates the purity of my intentions—to waive the question of payment. Work for love's sake was to be my motto. And, as an earnest of my good faith, the editor would herewith please find a set of twelve vignettes to cover a year's issue, January to December. There's a proverb about the slowness of the world to recognise genius. In *re* those vignettes, my line in the pure milk of literature was apparently not acceptable . . . so I had to alter my style . . . brief, to the point, strictly factual, masterfully compressed. Which, on reflection, must be accepted as the style of styles. . . . Editors demand austerity prose . . . we must be patient with them. We must make allowances. I do—and when they turn down one article, I submit another—a procedure known as turning the other cheek. . . . So here's a song. . . . You can make it a solo, if you like. I can't, as I'm but a *tutti* singer.

> *If you've got a thought that's happy,*
> *Boil it down.*
> *Make it short, and crisp, and snappy,*
> *Boil it down.*

When your brain its coin has minted
And the moral you have hinted,
If you want the effort printed,
Boil it down.

The Warrior claimed to be the first Army magazine to print anything by Frederick Coutts who shielded himself behind the Greek pen-name of Kappa. These early contributions commenced a relationship with the magazine which lasted more than twenty-six years. In 1953, a former editor of that magazine, the then retired Lieut-Colonel Madge Unsworth, was invited to write about 'Kappa' and his work through those years:

> Would this contributor prove too 'highbrow'? Certainly some of his illustrations were from the early philosophers. But in the same paragraph with them one came upon the keynote sounded in all that has followed: 'The great thing is to steep ourselves in the New Testament, until we are dyed with the thought of Christ through and through.' Readers asked for more. 'Kappa' changed to 'Ensign', whose imaginary 'Broadcast Conversations'—beginning with one on 'This Sanctification Business'—made all feel perfectly at home. . . . With facts irrefutable, with fun irresistible, with gentleness, firmness and respect.

'Kappa' was the beginning of something so extensive and influential that he could never have envisaged just what the ramifications of those first manuscripts would be for himself and a part of God's church.

In August 1926 Captain Coutts was promoted to ensign. In that there is nothing extraordinary: there were hundreds of ensigns in the Army then. But Ensign Coutts was to turn the rank into a *nom de plume* which gave articles a very special hallmark. If 'Ensign' had written it, it had to be read.

In *The Warrior* Coutts continued with a series 'From the officer's room' subtitled 'Unofficial Talks by Ensign'. These recorded conversations took place in the officers' room as 'Ensign' was waiting for a band or songster practice to begin, or just before or after a meeting. Matters affecting the attitude of young salvationists towards, or behaviour in, the world and the Army were brought into focus: love and marriage, relationships, giving and receiving criticism, being normal and being a Christian, candidateship, gambling, alcohol and smoking. Other matters of purity and honesty, wanting to leave the Army because the commitment of some salvationists was not up to standard, and the hardy annual self-denial financial appeal were carefully examined.

Series followed series. The settings and the form changed, but the general pattern remained: answering the basic questions posed by young Christians learning to live in a sometimes attractive yet always sinful world and the promotion of the salvationist's heritage and the movement's principles and procedures. The reader could identify himself completely with the problem. Later, for example, young salvationists at school and university were, because of the enormous acceleration of knowledge, facing the hotly debated problems of science versus religion. In 'Ensign' they had a champion: he had married a scientist. Coutts had made a special study of this peculiar 'tension' and in his collectanea there were many articles dealing with the subject. 'Please do not apologise for raising the subject. All these important points keep on cropping up again and again, and need to be thrashed out again and again,' he began one article, reflecting his own attitude towards the eternal questions as well as helping the new generations find the right answers.

A 'one ton' Ford, travelling at about twenty-nine miles an hour, was now needed to move Ensign and Mrs Coutts and their daughter and piano from Chatham to Winton on the south coast of England on 12 May 1927. Though exhausted they were determined to meet their soldiers at the welcome meeting on the day of their arrival. Their coming caused quite a sensation: the corps had not had young officers for a long time. Even the local newspaper reporter was mystified when he called at the quarters for the customary interview, for when Mrs Coutts answered the door she was greeted with the question: 'Is your father at home?' In the following edition readers were informed that a 'boy and girl' had taken charge of the local Salvation Army corps. The news soon spread that 'a couple of kids' had been appointed to Winton.

Mrs Coutts would captivate the Sunday morning congregation with her simple, effective Bible word, sometimes concluding with a solo which the ensign accompanied. In the salvation meeting the ensign would lead a chorus singing session and sometimes the prayer meeting, from the piano. There was no repetition in his sermons and his topicality made them attractive to listen to. Part of the secret lay in his illustrative material referring to current events and quoting from people not normally associated with the pulpit: H. G. Wells, Karl Marx and Voltaire. In an era when the world of the salvationist did not enjoy a happy union with the world of sport—no 'self-respecting' bandsman would dream of attending a first division football match—Ensign Coutts was using sport and sporting personalities to illustrate spiritual truths and to attract his hearers. Whilst his material was excellent his mannerisms when speaking in public were again a matter for comment: his nervousness was still evident.

One Armistice Sunday there was a united service held in a packed Winton cinema. Many ex-service personnel were present to hear a prominent and eloquent member of parliament speak about his experiences on the battle-field. This was to be followed by Ensign Coutts' Bible address. Coutts took his place before the congregation and taking a number of Bibles piled them on top of one another and asked the congregation to try and imagine that every letter, not just every word, in those books, represented a life lost in the past conflict. 'That is the real cost of war,' he declared.

He enjoyed the fun of corps life and helped to organise the 'socials'; evenings when people relaxed together, shared a meal and played games, of which his favourites were 'The grand old Duke of York' and one in which he took a leading part, 'Father Confessor'. As far as the corps programme was concerned, he was adventurous and prepared to take risks, a vision not shared nor always

40

appreciated by some of the soldiers. The programme had to change. So Warrington Band was invited for an Easter weekend campaign and the local cinema was booked for Good Friday meetings.

He caused a sensation by inviting the recently formed Salvationist Publishing and Supplies Band, under the leadership of Captain Eric Ball, to campaign at the corps. A visit by the International Staff Band, described by some as a hare-brained scheme, was another success. His 'specials' included the Staff Songsters and the Chief of the Staff.

The corps recognised it was in the hands of a slave-driver: there was no let-up. Many of the bandsmen were shop workers whose employment could end as late as nine o'clock in the evening, or later, when the streets were still crowded and the pubs full. In spite of working such long hours the men would take their uniforms and instruments to work and go straight to the open-air meeting at the Talbot Hotel, in Pine Road, in time for the pub raid at turning out time. They would then march to the hall for a meeting and there many of those brought in from the pubs would kneel at the mercy seat in tears.

A three-month long cinema campaign, when a local cinema was taken each Sunday evening for meetings, was just part of a thriving outreach programme. Cinema-going in the 1920s was still a sin in salvationists' eyes, and even for the non-religious there were no picture houses open on the Sabbath. So the ensign hired The Plaza knowing that people would go to 'the pictures' more easily than they would enter a Salvation Army hall. However he went beyond all reasonable limits when one Sunday afternoon he arranged for the projectionist to show the film of General Bramwell Booth's visit to Japan. Some soldiers were so upset that they refused to attend and the question of just what The Salvation Army was coming to, was hotly debated.

There was a crisis in the young people's work: there wasn't enough room in the present building, so the Cranmer Road Mission Hall was rented for ten shillings a week. Eventually it was necessary to launch a building scheme and so the whole district was canvassed for funds.

For this reckless venture the ensign received a severe reprimand from National Headquarters.

Lieut-Colonel Isely again visited Coutts in his corps and Senior-Captain Carvosso Gauntlett came to lecture on 'Hungary'. It is said that it is a poor man who cannot admire another, and Gauntlett admired Isely. How it came about that Gauntlett was invited to Winton is not clear, but if Coutts and he were not friends before that June weekend in 1927, they certainly became friends afterwards. Carvosso was the second of the two most influential people in Coutts' life. In fact he was to become one of the few people with whom Coutts enjoyed a deep friendship of like minds; of equals.

The qualities which united Isely and Gauntlett were many: their intellectual powers, their skill and discipline with words and their ability to communicate, especially with young people. They also shared an internationalism, a spirituality and a sacrificial life-style in the service of God and the Army. Both were totally loyal and dedicated salvationists.

Then there were two particular qualities which separated the two men. One was their personalities: Isley was shy and retiring; Gauntlett was an extrovert, fun-loving and open. As a lieutenant he had once sold copies of *The Daily Herald* instead of *The War Cry* in the village in which he was stationed—just for a lark. The second thing which separated them was their feelings towards Germany: Gauntlett loved all things German; Isley, because his feelings were so anti-German even refused to receive the German edition of *The War Cry*.

From Isely, Coutts had learnt 'the worth of a reasoned faith'; from Gauntlett he was to receive 'a vision of a Christian society which not merely defies but can transcend all human differences'. It is difficult to measure the impact of Gauntlett upon Coutts; but the most reliable indicator must be the tribute which Coutts wrote to the man he affectionately called 'Car'—a biography entitled *Portrait of a Salvationist*. As an inspirational testimony, it is a classic. It proves the worth of publishing the movement's history because the record of Gauntlett's exemplary life can do nothing else but encourage, inspire and challenge others to a deeper commitment to their Lord and Saviour. The content of the book suggests Coutts' worshipping of Gauntlett was just this side of idolatry. But then, when Gauntlett became editor-in-chief and literary secretary, his whole department felt the same way about him.

Carvosso Gauntlett was the son of pioneering Salvation Army officers whose generation knew what physical persecution was. At the age of five he travelled with his parents, his brother Caughey and his sister Elsie, to a new home in Germany. In his childhood and youth he met the great founding fathers of the movement and discovered that as far as the Christian is concerned there are no foreign lands and no man is a foreigner.

He had entered the training garrison in London in 1910 when eighteen years of age and had two corps appointments in England before returning to Berlin to work in the editorial department. There he became one of the foundation members of the German Staff Band. When the First World War broke out other non-Germans naturally left the country as quickly as possible, but Gauntlett left only after the security police had come looking for a fluent German-speaking Englishman who didn't want to leave Berlin because he had things to do.

Back in Britain, still a bachelor, Captain Gauntlett began a work amongst prisoners of war and internees which, though performed quietly, still seemed to scream his conviction that all men are of one blood and thus brothers. The Great War being over, Carvosso married a Danish officer, Adjutant Mary Jensen, at Hammersmith in 1919 and within a few months they were on their way to live in a one-roomed flat without heating in Prague to share pioneer work in Czechoslovakia. The only food for their Christmas dinner was just two fried eggs which were slightly off. It was impossible to buy potatoes, rice, or salt. These were years of sacrificial service. Gauntlett adopted a Franciscan way of life in which he was totally dependent upon his Lord.

In 1925 it was again a story of pioneering; this time in

Budapest, Hungary. Gauntlett had to learn another language. He couldn't always afford public transport and had to leave the letters for London, ready and sealed, on the table because there was no money even for a postage stamp. Neither was there always bread for supper. He was doing enough work for two men but 'did not have two men's strength'. The sacrifice and dedication began to take their toll but that was no problem for him because 'the Army was in the very marrow of his bones'.

Gauntlett read avidly and recorded in a notebook which books he had read, their authors and the number of pages. In 1928 he read eighty-two books. In 1950, as the territorial commander for Germany, in a land struggling to recover, he read eighty-nine books. In the years 1934, '35, '36 he was reading four new titles a week. His mind was lively—always wanting to discuss philosophical, theological or social problems. His spiritual and mental parish was the world. Gauntlett, as principled a man as ever lived, was Coutts' kind of man.

During the winter of 1928/9 there was great consternation in the Army world surrounding the calling of a High Council and the retirement of General Bramwell Booth; the effects were felt in the corps at Winton, too. Some salvationists left and it was only due to a great deal of loyalty and devotion on the part of others that the corps survived. A happier note was the birth of the Coutts' second daughter on 26 January 1929. Dedicated Isabel Mary, she was for some reason always called Molly.

Farewell orders arrived that May and the corps presented the ensign and his wife with a framed certificate, signed by the census board, in ornate copperplate writing, with a carefully painted border as a token of their appreciation for the leadership that they had given:

To Ensign and Mrs F. Coutts
The Winton Corps (Bournemouth) wish you every
success in the future where ever work in our Beloved
Army leads you. Will you kindly accept our warmest
thanks and appreciation for all the Blessings which you

have been instrumental in bringing upon our Corps.

Your addresses both to the Elderly and Young People will always remain in the memory of those who have been privileged to hear them.

We thank you for all the efforts you have put in, all your good work and services, and pray that God will bless you and yours in your future years.

Believe us, yours in the War.

Though Coutts quickly learned that not every plan which worked in one corps would necessarily be successful in another, a definite pattern did emerge in his corps appointments. He showed initiative and flair by inviting big names and famous musical sections. The visiting officers included Mrs General Catherine Higgins, Mrs Commissioner Emma Booth-Tucker, pioneer officers, officers with international experience or with a story to tell, and officers serving in other less well-known branches of Army work. Coutts knew that on average soldiers did not know much about the Army outside their own corps and he wanted to widen their horizons. He was proud of the movement and wished his soldiers to be well-informed about all that the Army was doing.

Coutts learned two further lessons regarding leadership. Firstly, 'not to denigrate those to whom I was responsible in the presence of those for whom I was responsible. I learnt in due course that this rule applies to all levels, and he who breaks it is almost invariably repaid in his own coin.' Secondly, he learned 'to honour the local officers and soldiers for their faithfulness. They stood by their corps for better, for worse.'

His conclusion about officership was simple: 'As a stool needs three legs to stand evenly, an officer needs three firm bases for his life's work. He must be a man of God, a man of the Word and a man of the people.' His constant plea was that corps officers should be as well informed and as well trained for their own work as those who listen to them on a Sunday were in theirs.

Following a year at Pokesdown where Mrs Coutts would sometimes don her cap and gown to sing solos in the midweek meetings, the Couttses moved to St Helier in the Channel Isles. From the island of Jersey 'Ensign' started to send his most famous contributions to *The Officer*, a privately circulated magazine for Army officers around the world. His was the most famous of all pen-names for several generations of officers.

'Monday Morning Musings' first appeared in September 1930. 'The writer of this new and interesting series of "Musings" on everyday pre-occupations of Salvation Army officers is a successful young commanding officer on the British Field', said the editor when introducing him to his readers. Certainly in Salvation Army terms the articles were hard hitting. His readers eagerly awaited the arrival of the next issue of *The Officer* because he was saying what others were experiencing. Without fear he dealt with all kinds of issues.

His criticisms of the movement and those in it were crystal clear; his cries for better communication and understanding of the gospel and his commentary on the life-style of the servant of God were plainly written. It is no wonder that 'Ensign' received such a strong following. He became a cult figure, a prophet.

It has to be remembered that Coutts was never 'anti-bands'. A corps officer who cannot get permission to go 'specialing' with his band and disguises himself as a bandsman in order to go away with his men for a weekend's campaign, as Coutts once did, cannot be accused of having a down on salvationist musicians. But paragraphs such as the following illustrate the sharpness of his pen:

Here we have composers writing and re-writing manuscripts; boards sitting upon the final transcript; musicians checking the printer's copy; bandmasters conning the score at home; bandsmen playing and re-playing some awkward linking passage in search of perfection. Hours will be spent upon a piece that will take seven minutes to play in the open-air—one which, with further music flowing in full spate from our printing presses, may not be played again for a couple of months.

In that same open-air [meeting], at the conclusion of the band piece, the leader will say, 'Someone now with a word of testimony.' Whereupon often some saintly old veteran will step in, or the officer, feeling that he must make an effort to redeem the situation, clutching at the last line of the last chorus like a drowning man at a straw, will splash round madly till all his appeal is lost in a froth of ineffective phrases. . . .

Were a tenth of the enthusiasm and laborious attention to detail that go to make up the glamour and *bravura* of an Associated Headquarters' Festival given to the powers of self-expression in the field officer, the face of The Salvation Army in Great Britain would be changed for the better beyond recognition.

But in this effort—the spearhead of the Army's attack upon our godless population—one feels that the corps officer should be assisted by Authority. When and where is he adequately instructed in the art of thinking, or of clothing his thoughts in telling language? The training college? . . . probationary lessons? Advanced training—those post-collegiate courses, as our *Year Book* handsomely styles them? . . . at the end of it he is thrown back on his own resources again.

For him, earnestness in communicating the gospel was not enough, neither did he see any magic in the repetition of certain familiar phrases.

He also wrote under his own name which had become Frederick L. Coutts—his taking the 'L' from Lee, his wife's family name; there were book reviews, articles about the necessity of reading, and about moral and social issues. He had discovered his own gift.

On Jersey, Coutts always took the opportunity to contact those listening to the corps open-air witness. He did this because it was from these conversations that he learned what was filling the minds of the people who were yet to be converted. The questions they were asking, their picture of God, their view of the world determined how best he could speak to them of God's love and mercy. He wanted to be sure that what he was saying was speaking to the people's real needs. This extremely reserved man had made it his business to talk to the unconverted for his own, as well as the gospel's sake. It kept his soul alive and his mind and spirit fresh. Staleness, complacency and boredom were things he fought hard against in his public ministry.

An important change took place in his public work whilst in Jersey. 'Some little time ago my private ambition changed. . . . I used to think that if I worked hard at myself, burnt the midnight oil, sat in the "wee sma' hoors", collected much material, took my platform opportunities seriously . . . God might reasonably recognise me as a profitable servant and impart to me the final polish—the presence of his Holy Spirit—so that men, duly impressed, would inquire of each other: "Who then is this faithful and wise steward?" . . . My ambition has now changed. I no longer expect to make an impression on any audience. I do not desire to. To have people leaving the House of God thinking of the things I had said or done would be sacrilege. . . . The result of apostolic work was that it sent men away pricked to the heart; not complimenting Peter upon the excellence of his oratory . . . but crying as those who found themselves well nigh lost, "Men and brethren, what shall we do?" . . . All I want now is . . . to fall back upon the almighty power of God; not, of myself, to impress any—but to remind them of Another. It is not I who hope to win men to Christ: it is God which worketh in me.'

And he knew there was more to being a corps officer than preaching; in those days there was also a great deal of collecting. Calling one day on a gentleman for the self-denial appeal the man was sure he had seen the adjutant before. 'Not on this errand,' Coutts replied. 'But I've given to you already. I recognise your face,' affirmed the potential donor. 'I accepted the compliment as meekly as my nature would allow, and murmured that while it was true that he had already given his annual Christmas donation, his annual young people's donation, his annual harvest festival donation, his annual donation to our senior band . . . yet it was another donation that I now had the honour of soliciting. . . . He took the explanation in the spirit in which it was proffered and produced his customary half-guinea.'

Other corps appointments followed in London and Scotland. Coutts was a good and 'serious' visitor though he was not beyond just calling into a house where he knew the woman was a good cook to see if there was any apple-pie to spare. At Leyton Citadel, where there were nearly a hundred staff officers of all ranks on the roll, the attendances increased and local clergy found members of their flock straying to hear the Army captain. Some voices were raised in criticism that his preaching went above their heads, but nevertheless, at times, people queued to get into the hall and seats had to be reserved for the salvationists returning from the open-air meeting.

Because of the positioning of the electric meter, it had become a game for the local lads to nip into the hall and turn the lights off at the mains whilst the meeting was in progress. It became less and less amusing and Adjutant Coutts decided something had to be done. Arthur Harvey, a young bandsman, thought that he was alone in the hall when carrying out the necessary work. On receiving an electric shock he voiced his feelings rather strongly. To his amazement he heard the voice of the adjutant who was quietly standing by the door: 'I think I've come at the wrong moment, Arthur. I'll leave you alone and hope all goes well.' His discretion and quiet manner made a far greater impact on the young bandsman than any long lecture on his vocabulary.

The soldiers at Leyton Citadel were also very sad to see him go. One salvationist suggested to Mrs Coutts that the adjutant should ask to stay on. 'He would never do that,' replied Mrs Coutts. 'He would accept it as God's will for us to go, whatever his personal feelings were.'

The Couttses took up a corps appointment in Edinburgh where they opened their home to William McAllister, a young Salvation Army officer studying medicine at the University prior to service overseas. Bessie willingly spent time helping him with his organic chemistry studies.

It was probably the move to Clydebank a year later which confirmed Coutts in his socialist views. There were still children without shoes, just as there had been when he was a boy at Leith. The poverty was great. His determination to stay in touch with the realities of the world was again evident as he regularly waited until the shipyards closed on a Friday night and then caught the workman's tram so that he could mingle with the men, some of whom looked out for him just for a chat. The results of these conversations could be read each week in the local press in a series entitled 'From the top of Kilbowie Hill'.

The Saturday night open-air meeting held at the end of the street in which the hall was situated was impressive. A band of forty men quickly captured the attention of the hundreds of people still on the streets and as the gospel message was proclaimed there were those who were converted as they knelt at the drum-head.

One Saturday evening a group of children stood listening to the salvationists. The adjutant approached them, talked to them, and then taking a bare-footed boy by the hand entered Marshall's shoe shop. They returned a few moments later, the child shod with new shoes. It was not unknown for Coutts to be up early to meet a man being released from a Glasgow prison to make sure all went well.

On 30 November 1934 the Couttses third child, a son, John, was born at Clydebank.

By this time Frederick Coutts had been 'noticed', his talents were needed elsewhere in the Army, and ten full, exciting and successful years of corps officership, which he had thoroughly enjoyed, drew to a close.

CHAPTER FOUR

As for me and my house

Considering the impact which his writings were making and the fact that the editorial and literary department at International Headquarters was always on the look out for new writers, it must have come as no surprise to anyone that Adjutant Coutts became a member of that department in May 1935. Here he could develop his innate gifts and be coached in the necessary disciplines peculiar to writers and editors. There was the added bonus of working with some very colourful and interesting characters, and receiving an endless supply of books to review and study. Because there was neither house nor furniture ready for them in London, the Couttses with their three children moved in with Bessie's brother Harry, and his wife Lena, who were officers stationed in Stratford, in the east end of London.

Mrs Coutts possessed many of her father's characteristics and had definite plans for her children: they were to be brought up by the sea. Accommodation was thus found in Station Road, Westcliff-on-Sea, Southend. Even though the flat exceeded the rent allowance and the travelling up to headquarters was more than allowed by regulation, the family still moved in. It was a small flat, a little way from the sea, with a minute kitchen and a large lounge; Margaret and Molly shared a rather pokey, windowless bedroom. Father, mother and John slept in the larger bedroom.

From the kitchen window it was possible to see the railway line and it was someone's job to watch out, and shout, when they saw their tall, lean father waving out of the window as the train approached the station: it was time to put on the kettle.

51

Once a week he would bring a parcel home, neatly wrapped in brown paper and tied up with string, containing the family groceries bought at headquarters. And every Friday evening, as regular as clockwork, Molly would go on her scooter to meet her father at the station to collect her twopence pocket money.

The family had to adapt to another kind of life. Coutts had his work but there was a large element of frustration for Mrs Coutts. Possessing a trained mind, having been a teacher, and ten years the wife of a busy corps officer, now she had no other responsibility apart from her family. If her husband was 'a platform person' then Bessie Coutts was 'a people's person'; she was much more approachable than he. Mrs Coutts had now the difficult task of discovering a completely new life-style for herself. Eventually people needing help, guidance and encouragement did find their way to that small flat.

Coutts became the corps sergeant-major at Southend Citadel and the children took their place in the young people's corps. Every Saturday night he put money in the children's cartridge envelopes and then cleaned all the shoes, setting them tidily in a row, ready for Sunday morning. His open-air work on the promenade was particularly effective, managing to catch the attention of the large crowds of mostly day-trippers with an introduction about the test match, the lifeboat, the pier or some current event. Before they realised it, the crowd was being held captive and hearing the gospel message.

Just before the holiness meeting Coutts would come in from the open-air meeting and in the junior hall make sure that his children were neat and tidy. Margaret, in her singing company uniform—white blouse with a hand-embroidered crest on a detachable Peter Pan collar—would be carefully inspected.

From the start, Daisy, the primary sergeant, had problems with John (a highly-clued-up lad) because he would constantly interrupt and correct her as she told a well-known Bible story. In the end John would be asked to tell the story himself, and he did. It was second nature to him.

The great thing about the Coutts family was that everyone had to do something; no one was allowed to sit on the sidelines. At the light-hearted Saturday night meetings the band would play, Molly would sing with her mother, Margaret would play the piano with her father, and John, who from a very early age learned poems and humorous pieces, would recite.

Coutts also organised special mid-week meetings and Songster Leader Brindley Boon, a musician and elocutionist, would frequently take part. Boon, who was working at the Men's Social Services Headquarters, would meet Coutts at the station so that they could travel down together to Southend. But there seemed little point to that part of the exercise for he completely ignored his guest for the whole of the journey, taking a book out of his case and losing himself in the text. The only exchange of words was as the train approached Westcliff-on-Sea Station: 'We get off at the next stop, Songster Leader Boon.'

Following the promotion to Glory of his father in 1926, Frederick's mother had made her home with Ernest back in Warrington. Ernest bought a house in Hillock Lane, Woolston, calling it 'MANDI' (Ma-and-I). By now he had become the head of the buying and the costing departments at a local steel works and was a very faithful local officer.

On Saturday 20 August 1938, after a long courtship Ernest married Margaret Fogg: they were very much in love. Frederick conducted the service. The reason they had waited so long to marry was that they had wanted everything to be just right. But their wedded bliss was soon to be shattered. Towards the end of June the following year, Ernest became terribly ill and took to his bed. A 'deadly serpent had suddenly reared its ugly head' in their garden of Eden. The finest doctors were brought, his employer even demanding and paying for a third opinion. Ernest's condition deteriorated and so professional nursing was arranged. His brother travelled from London to see him.

That following weekend Coutts was due to lead a weekend's meetings at Hull Icehouse. On arrival he told his hosts of Ernest's illness but nevertheless said he would fulfill the appointment. There was no telephone at the quarters nor at his billet, but during the night a message came to the home of the local Salvation Army Assurance Society officer calling Coutts back to Warrington where his brother was dying. He stayed to conduct the holiness meeting and then travelled westwards to his brother's bedside.

Ernest died at seven o'clock on Monday morning, the third of July 1939. Just thirty-five years old he had been married for only eleven months. As the funeral procession passed the factory gates which Ernest had entered so often, fellow workers from Ryland's fell in behind the march, and the several hundred workmen who stood around his open grave testified to Ernest's far-reaching influence.

This bereavement was a terrible blow to Coutts. Almost as if to exorcise his grief, there appeared in the January to December issues of *The Warrior* magazine of 1940 a serial about his brother's life. These articles carried only the initials F.L.C. Coutts presented Ernest's widow with a bound volume of that year's issues of the magazine, writing in the front 'In memory of one for whom we both cared. Christmas, 1940'.

Five years later, the episodes were published in a pocket-sized sixty-three-page-booklet entitled *Short Measure—Portrait of a young man,* by Frederick L. Coutts; price one shilling and sixpence. It was not his first book, but even by Coutts' standards it was special: no exaggerated adjectives, simple words and sentences, lots of humour, many hidden messages for the astute reader, and a very special insight into the feelings of two small boys who needed each other's companionship to survive the changes implicit in the lives of Salvation Army officers' children.

One of the most noticeable themes is an appeal to officers to realise that amongst their company of listeners are educated men and women wanting to hear something spiritually helpful that is related to the world in which they have to live and work—a word which satisfies not only the heart but the intellect. His appeal was for relevant preaching and a satisfactory proclamation of the doctrine of holiness.

Using Ernest as a mirror, he focused on 'the problem' of the young Army musician and his spiritual life:

As for the rest of corps activities, what was a holiness meeting compared with a tip-top festival? The one was dull and hesitant; the other bright and sparkling. One was full of words and phrases that sounded somewhat stuffy and certainly rather remote from reality; the other was vivid and alive. . . . Probably more than one young bandsman has experienced these feelings. . . . He just knows that for some indefinable reason the festival appeals while the holiness meeting appalls—and does not stop to find out the reason. . . . After all, if brass band artistry was more interesting than a devotional address, whose fault was that? Surely not his!

What was this holiness anyway? How on earth was a chap to relate that . . . to a world of cheap cars, loudspeakers, performances twice nightly, overspiced fiction, the products of Hollywood, the Association Football Final, and the Australians playing on the county ground?

Coutts never underestimated either the intelligence or the spiritual needs of his readers and listeners. The onus was upon the preacher to present his case in just as attractive and captivating a manner as the musician enthralled his audience.

One of Mrs Coutts' highest priorities was that her children should receive a good education; a vision equally shared by her husband: 'I hold no brief for such cheap words against education as are even yet heard within our ranks,' he wrote in 1931. 'I hope I may scrape enough pence together to give my girlies as much as they will need. But the production of a certain spirit, not the memorizing of facts, is what I am after. Breadth of sympathy is ever a true mark of genuine culture.

55

Education that alienates from the poorest needs correcting by the mind and example of Christ.'

He wanted every salvationist to be better educated, and was proud of every salvationist university student. He did not ask anyone to give up their intellectual progress, but he had little patience with those who, because of their learning, became aloof or took their place upon some high pedestal.

But the education of their children involved more than just schooling. Coutts took his two daughters to their first classical concert at Watford Town Hall. Both parents wanted to open their children's eyes to the best and beautiful and cultured things of life. Though neither Coutts or his wife were travellers in the tourist sense of the word, they were internationalists; their friendships proved this. However, during Easter of 1936 Coutts had received his first opportunity to travel abroad as a Salvation Army officer. Lieut-Commissioner Gustave Isely was the territorial commander in France when Coutts was invited to lead young people's councils at Ully-St-Georges. One boy had cycled fifty miles to be present.

The Couttses knew there was an important world on the other side of the English channel and though they did not cross that stretch of water every year, foreign holidays became an accepted part of their children's education. They stayed in Salvation Army holiday homes or simple, inexpensive Christian guest-houses.

But Coutts didn't only take his luggage, there was always his 'meths' stove because 'you never know when you'll be able to get your next cup of tea'. He brewed-up in the most dangerous of places, even in the railway carriage whilst travelling. When the train stopped he would dash to the nearest tap to fill his kettle, leaving the family in great anxiety lest the train should depart without him. And there were his books, of course.

A neat and tidy parcel containing review copies and other books he wanted to read, would be sent on ahead to their holiday address so as to be waiting for them upon their arrival. Even before the suitcases were unpacked the string was removed from the parcel and the books examined. Always with a pencil in his hand, he read widely and deeply, and not only books directly related to his work and the production of articles or sermons. This love of literature he passed on to all his children.

During the summer in which Ernest died, the family were holidaying in a very modest house called Maison Evangelique at Houlgate, in Normandy. All seemed peaceful enough where they were, till Coutts, listening to his radio heard the announcement of war. It was a question of getting back to Britain as quickly as possible and thereafter being faced with the need to seek another home for the family; the flat in Station Road was requisitioned.

The family was evacuated. Margaret moved to Mansfield to live with a miner's family called Frost, instead of beginning at the high school in Southend. Molly went to her Aunty Lena's. Coutts remained alone in the flat for a time and it was announced by the editor of *The Warrior* that because 'Ensign's' family were away, 'Ensign' was having an 'orgy of reading'. Fortunately the separation did not last long. By September 1940, the family were reunited in a large bungalow called 'Red Tiles', to be found in 'The Mall', in the village of Park Street, just outside St Albans. It was nearly a three-quarters-of-a-mile walk to the station and the family had no transport. It felt like the back of beyond and hardly any visitors came because it was so far from the beaten track.

The address belies the facts: The Mall itself was a sandy, unmade road; the large cold bungalow had no damp-course and no main drains; there was a cesspool surrounded by enormous undergrowth at the end of the garden. The positive aspects were that for a child it was a paradise: trees to climb and a world in which there was no limit for a lively imagination. But the huge garden had run wild. There was an apple tree which had gone the same way, so Mrs Coutts promised John that, if he pruned it, she would buy from him any fruit it bore. To his amazement the following year it was loaded with fruit.

Inside, the bungalow had everything except mod cons. As John lay in bed and looked up at the ceiling he saw a damp patch vaguely resembling a map of Africa.

Grandma Coutts moved into Red Tiles bringing with her a washing machine, and a wireless which Ernest had bought her so that she could listen to the news in Welsh. Ernest's wooden garage came as well. The neighbours watched in amazement as it was pieced together. It did have one unexpected use however when very occasionally John successfully pestered his father to come and bowl to him and they played cricket together against the garage. But that did not happen often. Coutts did not have a close relationship with his children when they were small. Not only in his writings but also at home he was economical with words. If he was enthusiastic about anything the children had done they heard that it was 'very acceptable'; the ultimate chastisement: 'Child, I take an exceedingly dim view of that.'

At the beginning of 1941, Mrs Coutts went away for a time and it never occurred to the children to reason why. Margaret, then fifteen years of age, received letters from her mother in which there were instructions about the garden but no hint of the reason for her absence. One letter included the description of a meal: 'I was interrupted in this to have my dinner. It would have suited you! Vegetable hot pot (no meat) and steamed pudding with treacle sauce. They gave me so much treacle that I scraped some off my plate and put it into a little pot in my cupboard to help down the bread and marge!'

Writing to the twelve-year-old Mollikins, Mrs Coutts offered no enlightenment why she was not present at Red Tiles, but there was hope: 'I don't suppose I will have the need to write to you again from Willersley Castle, but will be coming myself with all the news, which will be much better,' she wrote. Father Coutts, as ever, was silent on the matter.

The war was raging and because of the bombing, the children used to sleep on a mattress on the floor, under the bedstead raised on bricks. The theory was that if the ceiling came down this would provide some protection. One night Molly and Margaret thus safely tucked away saw their father folding himself up like a penknife to get

58

his head under the bedstead to announce that their mother was coming home at any moment and bringing them a baby sister called Elizabeth.

The girls had had no idea about the possibility of another member being added to the family and their parents had never spoken about the matter. Elizabeth had been born on 6 March 1941, fifteen days *before* that letter to Mollikins had been written in which her mother had hinted that she would soon be returning to Park Street. Even then, after having given birth to a girl two weeks previously, she had not indicated that fact to her children, and her husband had kept the secret, too. Mrs Coutts was then forty-one years of age. Elizabeth was one of the 4,000 babies born at Willersley Castle, in the Peak District, to which the Army's Mothers' Hospital had been evacuated for the duration of the war. Margaret had to grow up quickly, accepting responsibility for domestic affairs and the care of the younger members of the family.

There were moments of strain in their family life. John remembers the arguments. At home there were four children, and a grandma to be looked after. The house was full of strong personalities, including Grandma Coutts of whom even Bessie was in awe. Added to which Brigadier Coutts was hardly ever at home—and when he was, he was working. He left early in the morning on the workman's train and arrived home late at night. The children found it strange to see their father in anything other than his uniform.

He could be seen late in the evening buying a cup of tea from a coffee stall in the road just outside King's Cross Station. He stood with his hands around his cuppa and his portable typewriter between his feet. One salvationist was intrigued by this because on the station was a Salvation Army Red Shield canteen. The answer was simple enough, she discovered: 'If you want to contact people you must mix with them.' Before the war, he was also an instructor at the week-night Clapton Local Officers' Institute where he gave lessons on the Bible, its background and its history. He was rarely at home at the weekend and accepted invitations to conduct mid-week meetings in and around the London area. There was fire watching duty at IHQ, and he had been appointed as a member of the International Staff Band.

It might have been a strain, but there was still room for others in Red Tiles. John Cooper was a young officer working on headquarters. His appointment took him away from home a great deal and so his wife, who was very ill, had the difficult task of also looking after their small daughter, Elizabeth, alone. The small family had been bombed out of their home in Petts Wood, South London, and it had become a tremendous problem for them to find any kind of suitable accommodation. Certainly no one was interested in taking in a bed-ridden mother, with a small child just about to start school. They were pitched from pillar to post; always having to move on. However the Couttses opened their home to them for as long as they needed.

Unlike his two older sisters who played the piano, John, his mother decided, should learn to play the violin. He hated it and it was a great mistake as his mother later realised. The problem was that it set him even further apart from his peers. He inherited the sum total of his parents' intellect and was set apart because he was such 'a brain' and the swot of the school. His going to the Army and wearing a red jersey on a Sunday (which he tried to hide from his friends) set him even further apart; the violin was the last straw. It was a real burden for him. He was ragged by other children as he carried his violin case through the streets and even the bus conductors asked for a tune when he stepped on board. The only tactic he could implement was to drag his feet in practice until his mother, recognising failure, scrapped the project.

One brighter moment came for John when three five pound notes arrived for him from America. They were from Sam Baird, the brother of Catherine Baird, one of his father's colleagues in the editorial department. Sam had heard just how badly John wanted a bicycle and so sent him the money to buy one.

One important aspect of their family life during the war years, and just after, was when they visited various corps to lead meetings as a family. Packing up four children to travel by train to the north of England, the Isle of Man or Chatham, was a military exercise in itself. However, as John was an avid train spotter, he was in his element on such journeys.

His role in the programme was as elocutionist and would include excerpts from *Three men in a boat*. Molly was never very good on the piano, though made to practise very hard: 'Just one more time,' she would hear her father say. So Molly played her recorder and sang the alto part in duets with her mother who sang soprano. Father accompanied them on the piano. Their most striking rendition was of Tchaikovsky's song which, when translated into English, received the title 'A crown of roses'. Mrs Coutts would also sing excerpts from 'Messiah'. Margaret played piano duets with her father in which he took responsibility for the more difficult passages. The brigadier made a point of finding sacred words to classical melodies.

When Mrs Coutts spoke in meetings she needed only a few words which she had written haphazardly on a piece of card. But their father was a prophet without honour in his own country. If he repeated a topic his children quickly reminded him they had heard that one before. Margaret remembers hearing him walking about in the small room in which he worked rehearsing his sermons. He would go over them time and time again and when he stood up to deliver those words, it was literally what he had on the paper. His timing was impeccable and because his gift was to make the difficult teachings of the Bible easy to understand, people could remember years later what he had spoken about.

Whenever there were seekers in his meetings, which was more often than not, he made a point of writing a letter the next day to each person who had gone forward to pray. During young people's anniversary meetings in Hull Icehouse, a number of young people had made public decisions. Coutts left for London on the Monday morning and in the Tuesday morning post all the young people received a typed letter of encouragement from him. One of the group, Mildred Lee, in whose home he stayed on the weekend of Ernest's promotion to Glory, in 1939, received the following:

Dear Mildred,

I thought I would send you this note because I could put in a letter what I didn't get the chance of saying to you before I left. I am very glad that you came forward on your own on Sunday evening, and I hope that what then happened in your own experience is standing the test of your daily work.

Those of us who, like yourself, have the advantage of a good home, are bound to do all we can to try to help those who have not the same privileges. You can do that, at the moment, perhaps through the Guard Troop or with girls of your own age. And then, as time goes on, other ways of service will open up to you. The first and all-important condition of usefulness is that we are always obedient to God's voice, and do what He tells us to do.

As you know, it is not always an actual 'voice' that we hear. Sometimes it is a conviction that grows within us. Sometimes it is a feeling we cannot get rid of that we ought to do a certain thing or speak to a certain person. In these, and other ways, God makes known His will to us, and He will keep on telling us what we ought to do so long as we are obedient to Him.

I will always be glad to hear from you if ever you want to write. Meanwhile, don't forget to seek God's help in prayer every day.

Yours sincerely

(signed) F. L. Coutts

Molly was a gifted mimic and at home she would act out what her observant eye had seen in the meeting copying the actions of visiting (and especially older) officers. Coutts didn't like that and would put a stop to it, not angrily, but he had too much respect for his comrade officers to see them being made to look silly. Neither did he ever speak about his work, or his colleagues, in front of the children. There was never an exchange of headquarters gossip or Army politics in their hearing: neither the Army, its policies, nor its leaders were discussed in the home. Later as an international leader he never revealed the secrets of the council chamber. The children were not raised on a diet of commissioner stories nor in later life allowed into the inner secrets of Army administration.

In so many facets of the family's life Mrs Coutts was the driving force and perhaps it was because of her own outstanding achievements that she not only wanted her children to succeed academically but was also disappointed that none of her children ever took up science. At the age of eight, John was entered for a preliminary entrance examination for Watford Grammar School. His mother promised him a jack-knife if he passed; but that was one occasion when he was not successful. Margaret worked hard to achieve her degree. Molly attended University College reading geography with Chinese as a subsidiary. Her father's old Flying Corps jacket came in useful on field trips because she could put the large maps in the pockets. Besides all other clothing was still rationed and it was good material.

The three older children managed to finance their academic success by winning scholarships and working at the Post Office during the Christmas peak period and in the income tax office at Easter and during the summer.

After the war the Couttses could again travel abroad for their holidays. There was the regular pilgrimage by Coutts to Commissioner Isely who had retired early at the age of sixty because of illness and who was living in a beautiful house just a few yards from Lake Geneva. He was promoted to Glory in 1954.

When still only a young boy, John travelled alone on public transport to his pen-friend in France, and on another occasion to Bavaria to visit one of several German prisoners of war who came to Red Tiles for dinner after attending the holiness meeting in St Albans. Molly and Margaret also visited France, staying with members of the Booth family.

Here was a Salvation Army officer's family in which

everyone's talents were recognised and stimulated. The Couttses shared a vision with their children of education, culture, travel and the implementing of Christian principles in everyday life. No one was spoilt, there was no money for that, but they were given everything their parents could offer them.

CHAPTER FIVE

My tongue is the pen of a ready writer

'Ensign' became a backroom boy in 1935 and was to remain so for the next eighteen years. His ability as a Bible student had been recognised and so he was appointed to prepare the *International Company Orders*, Bible teaching material for the Army's Sunday-school work world-wide. 'I foolishly imagined that I was well acquainted with the Scriptures. I was quickly undeceived,' he wrote. 'I rapidly learnt that there was a world of difference between the preparation of an address on a self-chosen text for one of next Sunday's meetings, and working through the Bible book by book, avoiding no obscure passage and side-stepping no difficulty, so that its principal lessons became clear to the eight-year-old, the thirteen-year-old, the eighteen-year-old. It was this yoke I was required to bear during those years, but a most profitable discipline it proved to be.'

The 'backroom' itself was in the International Head-quarters of The Salvation Army at 101 Queen Victoria Street, an old business house in the city of London. The remains of loading bays were still visible at the rear but it had been in the hands of the Army for more than sixty years. The Founder had passed through its mahogany doors until his promotion to Glory in 1912. Rumour had it that because there had been so many alterations within the building—it seemed that if you wanted an office you made it yourself—it was only the electric wiring which saved the whole rabbit-warren-like interior from total collapse.

During those eighteen years his colleagues were of such

a stature that the group must be considered as unique. Each honed the others' mental and spiritual powers: personalities such as Alfred G. Cunningham, Carvosso Gauntlett, Ben Blackwell, Madge Unsworth, Catherine Baird, Bernard Watson, Pop Moyler, Reg Woods and Arch R. Wiggins. Later came such personalities as Brindley Boon, Eric Coward, Cyril Barnes, Will Burrows and Will Pratt. Whose life would not be enriched in such good company?

There was a restaurant at IHQ, for those who could afford the prices, but members of the literary and editorial departments adjourned to the 'Blue Room', where there were no tablecloths, to eat their snacks. It was there that Coutts learned to know such young officers as Erik Wickberg, Tor Wahlström and others who were later to assume positions of international leadership.

As quickly as possible after 'lunch' the group mustered on the top floor, in Brigadier Clara Becker's office, for lively and sometimes noisy discussion. Brigadier Becker, an officer who was born in Russia, had been involved in the beginnings of the Army's work there. The subject of the book *Translator Extraordinary*, she was a gifted linguist and responsible for the translation bureau. Although small in stature, tea-pot in hand, she ruled over the assembly and they enjoyed it. As they sat around her huge table exchanging ideas, they heard first-hand experiences of the Army in Finland, Hungary, Czechoslovakia; or Coutts on Kierkegaard, some of whose writings had been translated by Gauntlett for *The Officer's Review* years before they were available in English bookshops. Politics were not forgotten: Gauntlett, Coutts and Watson were staunch socialists, Blackwell a liberal. There was a great deal of laughter and sometimes, because the topics were so absorbing, they had to make up the time after normal working hours.

Coutts never said much but enjoyed these occasions immensely. At the end of some difficult point when they hadn't resolved the matter someone would ask: 'Fred, what do you think?' He would hum and ha and then looking down at the floor say what he thought. After that there really wasn't anything more to say. He was too modest to push his opinions even when people were saying the most extraordinary things. At the start he was uncomfortable when the spotlight was turned on him like that, and sometimes he suffered inwardly because he couldn't adequately express what he was trying to say. This was the first of the legendary and famous 'tea clubs'.

When the Second World War broke out, Baird, Woods, Blackwell, Coutts, Watson and Gauntlett took a pacifist stance. They were convinced that for believers to take up arms was inconsistent with the Christian faith. No one had the right to kill another human being, but pacifists were not so much tolerated as despised. Their views were thought to be synonymous with cowardice and disloyalty. In that respect certain members of the editorial and literary department became 'notorious' for their well-stated and articulate views. They were the object of cheap jibes by some who had never experienced the demanding struggle of hammering out a costly personal faith.

Ben Blackwell had thought through every aspect of his pacifist convictions; he had an answer for every question. The words of James Kirkup: 'No men are foreign, and no countries strange' were engraved in the heart of Gauntlett and were to cost him, and several like minds, dearly. He suffered again in 1939-45 all he had suffered during the years of the First World War when he committed himself to providing pastoral help to German prisoners of war and other internees. Nevertheless he involved himself in the same work again.

Frederick Coutts had seen war before and had discovered that militarism was contrary to his own essential nature and faith. If at first he had only an instinct towards pacifism, then it was confirmed by his friendship with Gauntlett. According to Coutts, Carvosso wore his pacifism on his sleeve and was the decisive influence upon him in these matters. In every aspect of his life Gauntlett allowed himself to be governed by this principle. And Coutts could not compromise a truth as he had perceived it.

This meant pain, misunderstanding and misrepresentation for Coutts. He was approached by many young men asking for help when they were called upon to face a tribunal and account for their refusal to fight for king and country. Some judges could be very tough on 'conchies' so Coutts never represented a young man without first meeting him in a searching interview and never before being totally satisfied with the youngster's integrity and Christian testimony. Once satisfied on these matters, Coutts offered guidance and support and then spoke up for the young man in court. The outcome may have been shared quietly with a colleague, but it was essentially not a matter for congratulation or condolence. Privacy was respected.

A letter from Coutts to H. V. Cattle, on IHQ editorial paper, originally dated 12 October 1939, and altered by hand to 6 November, reads:

My dear Friend:

For some days now I have felt a concern to write to all salvationists I know who have taken up—or shown a sympathetic understanding of—the Christian pacifist position.

For my own part, I am as convinced as ever that war and the teaching of Jesus cannot be reconciled. In saying this I gratefully acknowledge that The Salvation Army has publicly and officially recognised the legitimacy of our stand (see *The War Cry* for May 13th last, page 5).

It would be foolish to deny that we are but a small group. Let us encourage our hearts, however, with the thought that God is able to use us, not according to our numbers, but according to His power.

We must continue to pray for and keep in touch with one another. This we can do in a spirit of perfect loyalty to the international movement to which we are privileged to belong.

Sincerely yours,
(signed) F. L. Coutts, Major

War was not for him 'an unavoidable natural calamity like earthquake or flood. War [was] the cumulative result of the sin and folly of man. . . . What men [needed] to renounce [was] not this or that weapon of war but the principle of war.' He continued: 'We need mutually to repent of our savagery toward each other and, as the God and Father of our Lord Jesus Christ may help us, vow to live as one family around a common board.'

Speaking at Coutts' farewell from the department in 1953, Brigadier William Burrows referred to this commitment: 'We have seen him take the blast of the storm and be a shelter and a rock to those who could give him nothing.'

To add insult to injury those officers who held pacifist convictions were not only referred to as 'conchies' but the final mindless insult came when they were dubbed disparagingly as 'modernists', as if there was some connection between the two issues and as if the two words combined and represented some kind of common evil.

Of course not every one in the editorial department shared these views and that gave rise to tension within the work situation. At home, when his son John was in line to become a prefect at St Albans School, it was discovered that this could only be possible if John joined the cadet corps, a basic introduction to the armed forces. Coutts refused to allow his son to join.

On the night of 11 May 1941, IHQ was destroyed by fire. The amount of paper, the old oil-cloth and the matchboard partitioning fuelled the flames. The editorial and literary departments lost almost everything. Some members of the editorial department moved out immediately to St Albans, to be near the Army's printing house, Campfield Press. Others removed to an even more Dickensian building, a ramshackle warehouse at 224 Upper Thames Street overlooking the ruins of 101. The ground floor was uninhabitable and the head of the department, Colonel Carvosso Gauntlett, chose the worst of all the offices for himself much to the annoyance of his team. Coutts and Molly Akers, the young teenager who typed for him, were among those who moved over to '224'.

Coutts' workload increased. Apart from the *Company Orders* there was also the *Primary Manual*, corps cadet material, the *Star Card,* regular contributions to *The Officers' Review, The Warrior,* the Army's weekly papers, book reviews, pamphlets and anything else which came his way. Even his rough copy, typed with two fingers on an old machine, was impeccable: double spaced, wide margins with neat hand-made amendments. The whole was carefully scissored and pasted ready for Molly's final typing for the printers. Whatever the style and for which ever paper the material was intended, nothing was spoilt by careless spelling or imprecise punctuation. It was this same carefulness which marked everything he did in life.

If the air-raid siren sounded during the day they did not always go down to the shelters. Sometimes they ignored the signal, waiting until the planes were overhead and they heard a bomb whistling down. Only then would they dart to an inner wall for safety, and long before the all-clear was sounded everyone was lost again in the galleys or pages.

At night every city building was required to house a firewatcher who was to deal with the smaller fires which could start as a result of burning debris or red hot shrapnel. Though Coutts welcomed the pleasure of a solid, solitary evening's work, the empty, blacked-out rat-infested building with bare boards and a single electric bar fire for heating was no place for the faint-hearted. There was a singular lack of comfort: no easy chairs and only the facility for warming a drink.

One day, he rather diffidently asked Molly, his secretary, if she would do him 'a kindness'. His current reading included material that he wished to have on file and the page numbers had been noted. References should be set out so and perhaps she would then be kind enough to erase the faint pencil marks in the margins. Molly had reason to be grateful for being allowed to perform this kindness: 'Only much later did I realise his concern to guide my reading: biography, novels, poetry, biblical commentary, mystical writing, theological works of increasing depth. . . . His inner discipline, his insatiable intellectual quest, the breadth of his knowledge, the variety of interests which captivated him, his capacity for work, his creative use of every moment, the humility—that all this resided in one who was so approachable was a revelation to a teenager and brought deepening insights into what it meant to be a Christian. . . . I met an adult working man with a family who continued to read and work at himself, in addition to all his Army responsibilities and commitments.'

The first time that 'officialdom' had recognised him as an instrumentalist was in 1935 when he was appointed to play double bass in General Evangeline Booth's motorcade band alongside Albert Jakeway. During the war Brigadier Coutts took his place in the International Staff Band on the E*b* bass. He was a competent musician who could analyse chords and had a good ear. He was intensely interested in and had a deep appreciation of music generally. Apart from making a special contribution to the band by his gifted preaching, he also played piano duets in the programmes with young Don Morrison, as a change from Don's accordion solos.

On one occasion at Wembley Town Hall they played two duets at a grand piano. Because of the band's positioning on the stage the two played with their backs to the audience. As Coutts got more and more into the piece—there were several difficult passages for him—he began to push and by the end Don was sitting right on the end of the stool. Coutts had more or less taken over. Don was left just tinkering away at one end of the keyboard much to the amusement of the crowd.

Staff Bandsman Morrison was waiting to be conscripted and Coutts kept a fatherly eye upon him as he did with all young people caught up in war. Despite the bombing, the venues were always crowded with men and women in military uniforms who had travelled miles to hear the band: they were hungry for good music and a good word. It was as if people would queue just to hear a hymn tune. When Coutts spoke at such events he created a special atmosphere; he knew that some could be leaving that evening on a mission from which they might never return. It was if he was caring for them in some deep spiritual way.

71

As always with Coutts, there was no time to be lost even in the band practices. Whilst the basses rested and other sections were rehearsed, Coutts would pick up his proofs, correct what he could in the time available, and then put them down when the basses had to play again.

When he first arrived at '101', the editor of *The Musician*, Arch R. Wiggins, sent Coutts along to write a critique of one of the large festivals held in the Queen's Hall. He wrote a really critical article causing a sensation with his remarks, reminding some of musical commentator, George Bernard Shaw. Coutts was offended and puzzled by a section of a recently published piece by Phil Catelinet. Letter 'D' was a non-stop waltz based on the words, 'My burden at thy feet I lay, O Lamb of Calvary'. Coutts wrote that he really could not see the possibility of a seeker waltzing to the mercy seat to a non-stop waltz. 'When a penitent does that, he *staggers* up to the Cross. . . . I beg you not to forget the heart-break.'

Frederick Coutts was the salvationist musician's friend. Whilst aware of some of their shortcomings and the temptation to place music before mission, he never boxed their ears in public. Rather he always praised their work and commitment to God's Kingdom. He acknowledged the worth of their testimony at their places of employment and was as proud as any man could be to explain to a non-Army audience, or a press conference, the calibre of the men and women who play in Salvation Army bands. He just wished that all officers prepared for their public ministry as carefully as do the best Army musicians.

He never confessed to having a favourite Salvation Army band, but he did have special links with Chalk Farm. In the 1920s he had, via his father-in-law's friendship with A. W. Punchard, known something more than the average brass music fan about that band. Coutts' brother-in-law, Fred Lee, became a bandsman at 'the Farm' and Gauntlett was the band's tour leader on several occasions before his appointment to Germany after the war. With such connections it was hardly surprising that Coutts should be approached to be the band's regular 'leader' for its weekend campaigns throughout the country between

1947 and 1953. In between pieces on the march, Coutts would drop back to carry Bram Hughes's double bass, including one occasion when, in the pouring rain, the band took a short cut across a ploughed field at Sandwich where Lieutenant and Mrs Brindley Boon were the corps officers.

Eventually the editorial department was moved to the top two floors of house eight in the training college at Denmark Hill. The tea club was refounded on the top floor of house eight. After lunch in the health lodge on top avenue, someone would put the ancient kettle on an electric ring and make the tea. It was a happy group of like-minded people who had found a place where they could be themselves and discuss the things which meant something to them. Ben Blackwell, who had been a legal secretary before becoming an officer, knew how to weigh up the pros and cons and balance any argument. He was also the club's unofficial chairman. Bernard Watson was the bait: he was always sticking his neck out: on politics, literature, theology, social and ethical issues. It was honest and it was healthy.

The *International Company Orders* which Coutts edited between 1937-47 received excellent reviews from the British religious press. These books were used by religious knowledge teachers outside the Army, and even in internment and prisoner of war camps. Coutts wanted to bring the material into line with what children were being taught in schools and General George Carpenter said that Coutts had 'raised the standard of our teaching for young people to the highest peak it had hitherto reached'.

However the *Company Orders* which Coutts edited became the focal point of much criticism from readers and territories around the Army world—from people who were comfortable with a more literal interpretation of Scripture. Some territories considered writing their own material to supplement what was being offered from IHQ. One result of the constant criticism was that leaders began to be wary of the author. The problem was, however, that Coutts was cleverer than his critics. He was often able to answer them and their opposition to his material with statements from either the Founder, the Army Mother or

73

early Army writings. But be that as it may, he was a source of theological tension within the movement and London was constantly being confronted with this fact.

This response was nothing in comparison to the reaction of officers and soldiers alike when Lutterworth Press published *The Timeless Prophets* by F. L. Coutts in 1944. To many it was the wind of change blowing through the movement. It is difficult for later generations to assess fully the impact this 'simple primer' to the prophets of the Old Testament made upon salvationists of those days. Unexceptional now, his presentation of 'The Unknown Prophet of the Exile' challenged many readers whilst providing a great sense of release to questioning minds. Short, clear and simple it revealed his gift to make difficult Bible material become palatable.

Coutts did not write just to be controversial nor to show how much he knew, he was wiser than that. He did not wish to undermine anyone's faith, but neither did he believe that scholarship was opposed to building up faith or was the enemy of evangelism. He was convinced that to make the Bible intelligible people had to use the tools of scholarship. He never fell into the trap of pretending to be a scholar himself or giving the impression that he might know Greek or Hebrew by using the original words in public. Greek was for the quarters not the platform, was his motto. His theological study at night school and summer schools did not endanger his personal experience of Jesus as Saviour and Lord, but rather deepened it. 'My desire to see men truly converted unto God did not wane but burned more steadily,' he said. Like many mid-twentieth century Christians he inclined towards a warm evangelical heart coupled with contemporary biblical scholarship, and was animated by a strong desire to make the gospel an open book to the ordinary man. But all did not go smoothly.

Frederick Coutts and Ben Blackwell were appointed to the Doctrine Council; the latter as secretary and as a member. Brindley Boon was in Blackwell's office when the two returned from their first meeting. 'That's it then,' said Blackwell. The two had become involved in a debate which had so revealed their thinking that they were considered no longer suitable to serve on the council.

Slowly but surely an image was beginning to form in certain leaders' minds that Coutts was suspect. His pacifist stand during the war, his politics, his theology, his outspokenness and intellectual honesty, the fact that so much criticism was coming from abroad about the *Company Orders* and his writings, all confirmed the suspicions of the more conservative mind. He was a rebel and becoming a figure with whom many officers identified.

Strictly against regulations, some officers were passing on their copies of *The Officer* to allow their soldiers to read what 'Ensign' had written. He exerted a significant influence as he conducted meetings and rallies around the country, and the Students' Fellowship in particular held him in high regard. For his part, Coutts was the students' voice reflecting their ideas to the Army leadership. It was he who championed the cause of university education for officers.

In the autumn of 1946 Brigadier Coutts, representing the editorial department, travelled to the Netherlands and was witness to the re-establishing of The Salvation Army following its closure during the occupation. The Dutch edition of *The War Cry* reported his meetings in Amsterdam, Utrecht, Hilversum, and praised Brigadier Coutts for his clear pronunciation and perfect English grammar which made his sermons so readily understandable. He encouraged and enriched the great crowds who heard him in the open-air as well as indoor meetings. The reporter from Utrecht even thanked London and Amsterdam for the quality of the international 'specials' they sent.

In December 1946, Coutts took over the editorship of the privately circulated magazine for officers alongside his recently acquired responsibilities in an education and special work section of the literary department. To the world he appeared a gifted man who with great ease could communicate the most difficult of ideas, but he once confided to Captain Moon, a fellow editorial: 'You know, Gladys, I am not fluent, not by any means. As for the stuff

I write I really have to work at it.' No one must imagine that from the start Coutts was some kind of literary genius who because of his natural ability needed no training in the art of writing.

He owed much to Commissioner Alfred G. Cunningham who was the editor of *The Officer* when he submitted his first contributions to the magazine in the 1920s and was later the head of the literary and editorial departments when Coutts arrived at IHQ. It was Cunningham who heavily scored Coutts' efforts with the blue pencil, in the beginning: 'I owe much to him for his wounding, if not at all times tender, it was always the faithful wounding of a faithful friend.' Good writing demands discipline.

'I have no magic potion which, when taken three times daily, will transform anyone into a writer of such outstanding skill that editors will crowd his door begging on bended knees for the privilege of publishing his great thoughts. I have no formula—I never have had—nor will I ever have—any kind of formula which, breathed over an empty sheet of paper, will cause words of imperishable wisdom to fall thereon like manna from heaven. . . . Basically, what makes a writer is the same as makes a speaker, or, in another art, a composer. He has something to say. If a man has nothing to say, let him say nothing. My own approach to the work of writing is regrettably ordinary, ordinary in the extreme, and relies upon the determined application of the seat of one's pants to the seat of one's chair. . . . Writing, like speaking, is not a matter of stringing words together but of communicating an idea which demands to be made known . . . as Jeremiah said . . . "a burning fire shut up in my bones".'

When he had used the pen-name 'Ensign' for nearly twenty years one of his 'candid' friends suggested that he change it. 'What you need to give your stuff life,' he was advised, 'is a new, 100 per cent, hit-you-in-the-eye humdinger of a pen-name.' After a lengthy and humorous discussion with himself on paper for his *Warrior* readers he reached the conclusion: 'No new pen-name could by itself improve the quality of my work. . . . It's fire in the belly and ideas in the head that alone make any writing worthwhile. Let those be in evidence—and the name matters little.'

He never derided the essential knowledge of grammar, sentence construction and punctuation but knew that no amount of expertise ever put ideas into a man's head. 'Only the writer can give birth to the idea which is why, if an idea occurs at two o'clock in the morning, turn the light full on, ignore the protests of your wife, and don't turn the light off until you have got every word of it down on paper. Forget the enemy of your mind who would whisper that you'll remember it in the morning. You will not. . . . That magical phrase which visited you like an angel in the night no more knocks at your door when morning has broken.'

His basic rules for writing were:

1. I have something to say.

2. The words I employ should clearly convey the meaning of what I want to say. What is not clear in my own mind before I put it on paper, or say it from the platform, will not be clear to my readers or hearers. Clarity is a condition of effective communication.

3. To this end I will use the simplest words I can and as few of them as possible. . . . Few and simple words is the rule of all good writing. It is my sorrow when in the Army's press I see poverty of thought veiled in pompous language.

And his own protection against the acid article was to take over a maxim of Brengle and never commit words to paper without knowledge, without necessity, and without love—especially without love.

His own style of writing and preaching is immediately recognisable: he can be heard speaking as he is read. Those who observed him most closely assessed his preaching as a mixture of the Bible, and the *Manchester Guardian* in which even the cricket column was considered an essay in English prose. He needed no convincing that every writer needs an editor and always asked another to read his material. Often he handed copy over to people less experienced and less gifted than he, and expected a critical and honest answer. No one profits by 'yes' men, least of all a writer: it was his best friends who pointed out his weaknesses and failures, he often said. 'Only the unconscionably conceited will object to having his mistakes pointed out,' was his confirmed opinion.

He was never satisfied unless he was convinced that his argument was crystal clear or the facts completely accurate. And those qualities were manifest in his work only because of his absolute concentration. Whenever someone entered his office he was at work. He looked up and then concentrated himself fully on the person and the matter in hand. When the business was concluded, he was completely immersed in his work again, even before the person leaving had reached the door. Whoever he was, the speaker received the utmost attention.

But as an editor, which role demands quite another skill from that of a writer, he had to learn to correct others and accept alteration and correction from those above him who read the proofs: the literary secretary, the Chief of the Staff, and the General. Gauntlett, his predecessor as editor of *The Officers' Review* had helped get many 'Ensign' articles safely through that stage of correction: now he had to do the same for others. If it was a matter of correcting those who worked for him, and there was a question regarding style, facts or information he would begin: 'Put me right if I am wrong . . .' or 'Shouldn't this be . . .?' Of course it should be or he wouldn't have asked in the first place. He remained reluctant to deliver straight from the shoulder in a work relationship, either to colleague officers or typists: he was sensitive to their feelings and wanted them to save face whenever possible.

The editor's dilemma which he now experienced was crystalised in a letter to Colonel Erik Wickberg in connection with an article the colonel submitted for publication in *The Officer* in 1950. Coutts pointed out: 'There are two "external"—or so I think of them—factors to keep in mind when writing on a topic like this. One is the reaction of those above: the other that of those below. We have to phrase what we want to say in such a way that it will pass the eye of those who censor all written material; on the other hand we do not want so to water the truth down as to make it useless to those whom we wish to help.'

As editor of *The Officer* he continued to write pieces which forced his readers to face facts about Salvation Army life and practice. The essential principles of Christian discipleship were brought into focus and spiritual help was offered—just as the Founder had intended the magazine should do. Coutts promoted and generated interest in Army history and Army publications, and kept the world-wide officer corps informed about what was taking place in other territories than their own. The magazine was like a house with all the windows open; there was fresh air blowing through its pages.

Leading weekend meetings was a normal activity for the members of the editorial and literary departments, but no one 'specialed' more consistently than Coutts. If he could, he would be away every weekend: sometimes with a band, sometimes with his wife, occasionally with the whole family, mostly on his own. Corps anniversaries, youth councils, student fellowship weekends, instructional conferences and refresher courses, the variety was anything but boring.

All journeys, however near or far, were undertaken on public transport. Often it meant leaving home on a Saturday morning and returning on Monday night because he had gone straight into the office on Monday morning. During the week he would be leading a holiness meeting here and a Bible study there. He was also a teacher in the evening classes organised at National Headquarters. This kind of life was his meat and drink. He was rarely at home. He had so many friends up and down the country who regularly invited him to their corps that, apart from him being popular as a speaker, it must be concluded that he performed a pastoral role to those who invited him. His analytical mind, his spiritual sensitivity and modesty made him, at grass-roots level, one of the most liked people in the territory. Intelligent young officers drank in his conversation. And if he didn't speak much—he certainly listened well.

He possessed the common touch, knowing what lived in the heart of the people and reaching it. He went time and time again to the same officers and the same corps until his visits had the atmosphere of a reunion. It seemed he never forgot a face and hardly ever a name except for one person whose experience is firmly written in Coutts folk-lore. A man approached Coutts as if an old friend and began to make conversation. Coutts couldn't remember the man's name and not wishing to embarrass himself or the man, employed his usual trick in this situation. 'Tell me again, how do you spell your name?' he asked. The man, with staccato spelling replied angrily: 'B.E.L.L., Bell.'

The unexpected was never far away. Coutts recalls: 'One Sunday afternoon during the Second World War I was standing in our hall at Camberwell. There had been a near enough miss to make the building unusable, so chairs were scattered in disorder and dust lay thickly everywhere. I was surveying the melancholy scene when the street door opened and a file of people entered hesitantly. It was plain they were on unfamiliar ground. Finally one of them spoke up. 'Cap'n, would you christen the baby?' and he pointed to the child carried by a young mother.

'Hurriedly I cleared a space in front of the mercy seat, read from the Scriptures, gave thanks to God for this new life, called the baby boy by his name, and gave him back to his mother. The man who acted as spokesman was so uncertain as to what next should be done that only with difficulty did I dissuade him from passing the hat round. But what on earth persuaded those people, living in that spiritual wilderness . . . to put on their Sunday clothes and come to a half-derelict Salvation Army hall on the off-chance that they might find someone to return thanks for a new-born baby? They could be written off as theologically illiterate . . . yet they felt an overwhelming compulsion to acknowledge the God who is not far from any one of us.'

His mannerisms whilst preaching had now become as well known as his ability to preach: running a finger inside his collar, stroking his head, buttoning and unbuttoning his tunic; burying his face in his outstretched palm for several seconds as he considered his next point. But however distracting his mannerisms were, he received important invitations to preach at lunch-time services in some of London's most prestigious City churches, and people came to listen to him, too.

At a divisional holiness meeting at Highgate another side of the shy reserved Coutts was revealed. Hall and gallery alike were packed as usual and he had glanced once or twice at a couple of callow and frivolous youngsters who were competing with the meeting leader. He began to preach. At the first interruption, as they began to speak loudly to each other, he paused mid-sentence and waited for silence. He resumed his sermon, but they received no second chance. 'If your behaviour were directed only at me,' he said, 'I should try to ignore it. But I am here as Christ's representative and you will not insult his gospel in my presence. Please leave.'

The constant determination to keep informed about the concerns of the unsaved paid dividends. His interest in them was real, no role-play. At Campfield Press, where he was on Christian name terms with the men on the stone, he was totally accepted. He was a firm favourite leading the weekly lunch-time service with 200 workers around the presses. Two such series of meetings concerning the Ten Commandments and the Lord's Prayer were published in *The War Cry* as a series and then as small booklets. They are examples to others of his own precious principle that Christian truths can be attractively translated into the language of the non-churched.

When necessary Coutts displayed his interest in people in more practical ways. Brindley Boon was a member of *The Musician* staff under Ben Blackwell and it was recognised that he could advance no further in responsibility without becoming an officer. What Coutts did not know was that Brindley had applied three times for training and had been turned down each time. The problem was that Brindley and his fiancée, Nina, had been courting a long time and wanted to marry first but married couples were not encouraged to enter the training college. Songster Leader Boon and his bride-to-be had accepted that fact, married, and with great sorrow recognised that the door to officership was then closed to them.

One morning, following a prayer meeting in the editorial department, Coutts talked to Brindley about officership, listened carefully to the story and somehow started the wheels turning, even though the couple were over age. Boon applied again after an interview with the Chief of the Staff, Commissioner John J. Allan. At the eleventh hour the Boons were accepted.

After the close of the Second World War Carvosso Gauntlett returned to Germany as territorial commander. On being told of his new appointment Gauntlett asked that he should not be promoted to lieut-commissioner above other German officers whose junior he had been many years before. The request was honoured—for a while.

When the Deutschmark collapsed he took the same salary as a captain: he did not wish to be treated differently from anyone else. There was enormous poverty and the food parcels sent to him for personal use would be shared with others in need. He had a beautiful spirit and was described as a holy man growing ever more like his Master. He worked such long hours that sometimes he was too tired to carry his bag up the several flights of stairs when he returned home in the early hours of the morning.

An unexpected relapse following routine surgery caused the promotion to Glory of Carvosso Gauntlett on 22 September 1951. A few days later Lieut-Colonel Coutts arrived in Berlin to conduct the funeral service of his friend. Coutts had no money with him, much to the amazement and disbelief of the customs men who had not heard of salvationist hospitality where no money is required and still a man has all he needs.

The funeral procession made its way to the same cemetery to which Car had travelled more than forty years before in 1904 when as a boy he walked behind his mother's coffin. Commissioner Gauntlett once wrote to his second son Sidney: 'I think you know I am not narrow-minded or imagine that the Army is the only good thing. I don't think there are many who know its failings as intimately as I do. I've had exceptional opportunities of observing—*but I still think it's the best thing.*'

Coutts had described William Booth as 'The first salvationist' and his book about Gauntlett was entitled *Portrait of a Salvationist*—he had no higher accolade to bestow on anyone than that of 'salvationist'. The funeral service, and in particular the words of a British officer serving in Germany, made such an impact upon the commissioner's eldest son Caughey, and his wife Marjorie, that an earlier calling to officership in 1939 was re-awakened and confirmed. A day or two later, before they had had time to act upon their decision, a letter arrived. 'Dear Caughey and Marjorie, I 'opes as 'ow you won't take this enquiry amiss, but . . .'. It was Coutts wondering whether they had thought anything more about that call to officership they had heard twelve years earlier. Within three months they had left their children in the care of others in the family and found themselves at Denmark Hill training to be officers. Some thirty-five years later, as the Chief of the Staff, Commissioner Caughey Gauntlett, conducted the funeral of his father's friend, General Frederick Coutts. That 'almost hesitant and informally worded letter' was 'the direct word of God' to them.

Coutts' writings were reaching their target and being reprinted in other editions of *The War Cry* around the world. Between 1942 and 1951, thirteen book titles had appeared over his name apart from his work on the *International Company Orders* and for *The Officer*. He had an intuition about a small story he stumbled upon, a quotation, an incident, a fragment of Army history and could see in it some hidden potential for an inspirational story. He had a sixth sense for human interest stories. Many of the smaller books he wrote then, and articles he later published in retirement, were the result of that instinct.

Despite everything some leaders were still suspicious of him and his promotion was slow in coming: he was going nowhere fast. Then General Albert Orsborn played a master stroke. In the autumn of 1952, Coutts was sent to America on a two-month, coast-to-coast, preaching tour. It was a calculated risk as far as Orsborn was concerned because Coutts needed another image than the one he had—especially in the States—before he could be 'brought on'. To enable Mrs Colonel Coutts to travel with her husband, eleven-year-old Elizabeth their only child still at home, went to stay with Margaret and her husband, Ray, who were in the first weeks of their marriage.

One group of Americans collapsed with laughter when they heard that the colonel and his wife cycled to their corps at St Albans on Sundays. Of course his preaching and lectures made a great impact, but most significantly there was that mixture of Isely and Gauntlett. This was seen in his acknowledgment of the welcome he received at a united crusade luncheon at the Richmond Youth Centre. The applause died away: 'Ladies and gentlemen: It is extremely kind of you to welcome me, who am a comparative stranger to you, in this very warm way. And I take your welcome to be not any kind of tribute to me personally, for that of course, in the very nature of things, it can hardly be. I take it however primarily as your tribute to the organisation, The Salvation Army, in which I have had the honour and privilege of being an officer now for over thirty-two years.' He then introduced his talk with an illustration from American Salvation Army history.

Colonel Coutts went, he preached and he conquered—if not totally, certainly enough to be promoted. Eight months later, Lieut-Commissioner Frederick L. Coutts was appointed principal of the International Training College. He had left the 'backroom' for ever.

CHAPTER SIX

The way of holiness

Geographically it wasn't all that far from the office of the literary secretary in house eight to the office of the training principal on the second floor of the main building at Denmark Hill but in matters of responsibility they were light-years apart. The Couttses said farewell to 'Red Tiles' and with twelve-year-old Elizabeth moved to 1 Brantwood Road, South London, quite near to the college. During the next four training sessions nearly 900 cadets would be influenced by his preaching and his example of Salvation Army soldiership.

Coutts found the amount of administration in which he was now involved irksome: though well aware of his inadequacies in this realm he was not content merely to 'get by' but worked hard to master the skills and techniques required by his new responsibilities. He wanted to get nearer to the cadets and take a personal hand in their training. During private study periods the commissioner would make his way across to the men's houses knocking on a door here and there asking the cadets how their study was going and offering what help he could.

It was common practice for a principal's secretary to draft meeting plans for the commissioner which, after being agreed, received their final typing. But the new man prepared the whole programme himself, choosing every song and each tune with equal care. Captain Grace Garner had the impression that the new principal had never had a proper secretary before: he gave her such little work and was even typing his own letters. The captain, however, preferring to be kept busy, asked the education department for work. When her new boss discovered she was typing for someone else he wanted to know why. 'You're not giving me much work, commissioner,' she replied, 'so I asked them for some.' Though after this confrontation Coutts gave his secretary more work, the problem was not yet completely solved.

The captain approached her principal again: 'Excuse me, commissioner. I hope that people don't think that some of those letters going out have been typed by me.' Whereupon he coloured—and got the message. Coutts did not enjoy dictation and so typed his letters on scraps of paper which other people would have thrown away, edited what he had written and left them on her desk. From these small notes Captain Garner typed the correspondence. He didn't ask his secretary for help either; she had to anticipate or discover if and when he needed any assistance. He never rang the bell summoning her to his office except when he was on the telephone and needed something urgently. Usually he would go to her and ask: 'Could you spare me a minute, captain?'

The number of college officers under his responsibility and his working relationship with them was also vastly different from that in which he had revelled in the more intimate setting of the literary department. The college staff was neatly divided into departments: men's side, women's side and education. Two chief side officers and an education officer looked after the training of the cadets and the general secretary's department took care of the day to day administration. The frontiers erected by tradition and experience were crossed only by the brave or reckless. There were many 'political problems' relating to 'the sides' which did not promote a supple working together. This administration came between him and the more than 200 cadets in each session.

Everything was done to keep 'the sides' apart. The women cadets had to say each week where they would be spending their free time. This information was not required of the men. Thus a difficult situation arose when a woman cadet put down that she would be visiting a football match that had been arranged between the men cadets and college and training corps officers. She was told her request could not be approved. In response Cadet Arnold Bennett appealed to the training principal. As a result, not only were the women cadets given permission to attend the match, but the commissioner kicked-off the fixture.

It would have been easy if all the tension caused could have been resolved so easily, but the problems were more serious and deep-rooted than that. Above all Coutts was anxious to up-date the cadets' training programme and standards of education. He wanted to bring it into line with the age the cadets were to serve: banishing old-fashioned memory aids in doctrine lessons and finding more contemporary and more suitable methods of teaching. He was absolutely convinced of the need to train corps officers to the highest of standards. More than twenty-five years previously he had as 'Ensign' indicated the importance of the role of the corps officer and discussed the needs of their training. The responsibility was now in his hands.

He knew that all too quickly some younger colleagues looked for an escape from the pressures of being a corps officer, so he spoke about it. To those who said they were being called 'out' of officership he suggested that if their new calling brought less security, a harder life, and heavier cross bearing, it may well be that God was calling them to another avenue of service. But if by leaving officership their life would be easier, more secure, then they ought to examine their motives again. Another argument offered was that of being better able to serve God as a soldier in a corps—he never understood nor accepted that idea. Neither did he understand 'frustration' as a reason for leaving. Did 'frustration' really mean 'not getting your own way?' or 'things were not going very well?' he asked. 'Your calling is holy for God has called you. Your calling is difficult but God will strengthen you. Your calling is rewarding for Christ will be glorified in you,' were his words to one session.

However Coutts also recognised that resignation was not the only escape young officers sought from the pressures of corps life. He had seen that, too, in the 1930s. One of his contemporaries had started attending shorthand and book-keeping classes because his eye was 'fixed upon an office chair' by which he would escape 'the peculiar strain' which was his. 'I do seriously counsel my friend and all who privately share his intimate desires, that they had better bury these secret hopes forthwith and shed no tears over the unmarked grave. . . . Opportunity to put double entry into practice will not bring such ecstasy that we know not whether we are in or out of the body. . . .' Neither was he convinced that every bright corps officer should be moved away from the field because he was good or successful: ' "Too good to be an ordinary parish priest," said a dignitary of a promising ordinand in the Church of England. . . . In short, too good for work which corresponds fairly accurately to that of an Army officer. Now here is the delusion—not ours alone, but common to many movements—that the best men are too good to waste on the basic work of the organisation. In other words any duffer can dig the foundations but what brains and brilliance are to hand must be kept to shed a halo of light about the entrance hall.'

For Coutts there was no promotion from 'the pulpit'. He wanted to make sure that the cadets were fit to meet the needs of the people and the pressures of the work. He caused havoc by wishing to hear at first hand what was being taught to the cadets, and his desire to sit in the lecture hall and classrooms to discover for himself what the cadets were hearing, from whoever, was fiercely opposed. Coutts encountered considerable difficulty in gaining access into lecture hall and classroom for this purpose. There was more to follow.

Each cadet was obliged to keep an outline book in which he or she stored her sermon material. This material was marked by officers who offered criticism and helpful advice. Coutts wanted to see the books; this time not to read what the cadet wrote, but to measure the quality of the marking and read the criticism made by the officers. By a roundabout route, without the knowledge of any officer on the staff, Coutts obtained a selection of outline books, bringing out a report as a result of what he had seen and specifying what he expected in the future from the instructors. The new commissioner was making his mark.

As a matter of policy, each cadet was interviewed by the principal at least once in the training session. For most, that encounter constituted a never to be forgotten experience: they were more like spiritual tutorials. The cadet took his or her sermon outlines along and these became the basis of the conversation. Whenever Coutts discovered a spelling mistake he asked the cadet if he might be allowed to correct it.

Cadet John Larsson had just read *Natural law in the spiritual world* by Henry Drummond and prepared a sermon on the basis of what he had read. Coutts fixed on that outline and went through it point by point, nodding and humming. He asked for the thought behind each point, creating the impression that he was learning from the great truths being presented by his junior. For the married cadets, the interviews were described as 'a Christian family man counselling adopted sons and daughters'. Each interview closed with unhurried fervent prayer for family and loved ones, and a handshake.

Because there was little freedom for the cadets they had to find ways of letting off steam. One of the commissioner's lectures was on Army music, and for this a few men cadets decided to create a honkey-tonk piano by putting cutlery in the instrument. When the pianist struck up for the singing of a song which traditionally started all lectures, the proceedings dissolved into laughter. The principal smiled and requested: 'If any of you would like to see me about this afterwards, please come to the office.' A small deputation duly arrived wondering what their fate would be. However the cadets hadn't got the message. Other pranks took place and again those responsible were asked to appear before him. The tone was still fatherly but very firm: 'Lay off, lads, lay off.' And they did.

It was not the only time he was to show his displeasure. It was traditional to bring candidates in from the London area to one of the Camberwell Thursday night holiness meetings in which they would take part. One young man came forward to testify and began rather pompously: 'I stand before you as a mere stripling youth of seventeen.' As one man the session collapsed into gales of laughter. Gradually, the commissioner half-turning in his seat, looked at the cadets. He had not quite made a fist, but his fingers were squared at the knuckles and he was making small, hammer-like movements, rather like a woodpecker, on the arm of the chair. Becoming aware of this, the cadets stifled their laughter.

On Fridays, the commissioner's lecture began immediately before lunch prefacing the cadets' free time. That Friday Coutts stood slowly to his feet: 'I never again anticipate being shamed by a session of cadets as I was shamed by a session last night,' he said. Once he was so disappointed in the overall standard of the cadets' examination results that he let the 200 members of the session know that they had under-achieved. In the following lecture he apologised if he had unknowingly offended anyone by this comment.

For the past eighteen years Mrs Coutts had had to find her own avenues of service for which two 'official' sources of fulfilment opened up to her. First she represented the Army on the central committee of the National Council of Women. Second, and more important, was her interest in The Salvation Army Students' Fellowship of which she had been vice-president since its inception. Her membership card, made out in the name of B. Coutts, dated her associate membership from 7 January 1949. The aim of the group was to unite students at universities and colleges in Christian fellowship and service under the flag of The Salvation Army.

To put such a group into perspective it has to be said that in those days it was unusual for salvationists to attend university. Amongst officers it was generally only those with special training such as medical missionaries who were degreed people. However the change in the 1944 Education Act made it possible for the sons and daughters of the working classes to attend university. This brought new challenges into corps and salvationist family life: few had had experience of this phenomenon and its consequences. Young people were leaving small town and country corps for the first time in their lives to study in large cities such as London and Manchester. They needed protection and guidance: a fellowship in which they were understood and accepted: a base to which they could repair when university life threw up real problems of faith, witness and conduct. The student also needed help to cope with the attitudes of their fellow soldiers when they returned home as changed people.

Mrs Coutts wanted to establish a national framework of fellowships, despite the criticism of élitism, and the suspicion which this would arouse in the minds of those not privileged to have had a higher education. She did everything in her power to help these young salvationists—from meeting an overseas student at five o'clock in the morning to organising fellowship holidays on the continent. Her ministry of letter writing was of enormous importance and the fellowship magazine was anything but dull. Her husband kept a low profile in these activities, except for those occasions when he was invited to speak at their meetings or weekend conferences. Then he relished the opportunity to address such a lively crowd of young intelligent salvationists of whom he was extremely proud. Or in the more delicate matters when the fellowship needed guidance because of its attempt to air certain problematic subjects he was the astute Army politician and counsellor.

Once more after nearly twenty years Mrs Coutts had a definite role to play as the training principal's wife and she and her husband were able to work together again as a team—although a limited one. Mrs Coutts taught a remedial English class for cadets needing to improve their grammar, and formed a fellowship for the wives of training college officers. However, her special concern was for the married cadets who in those days were not allowed to take their children with them to the training college. The children had to be boarded out with friends or relatives for the whole of the session and naturally that brought much heartache and tension, especially when a child was ill or fretting for mother and father. At the end of one session Lieut-Commissioner Coutts sent a personal gift to all those children. At regular intervals throughout the training year he had been putting saving stamps onto cards bearing each child's name. It was a personal project from his own pocket and had nothing to do with the college.

When news arrived that the father of an overseas cadet had died, the principal, knowing she would soon be out of class, wandered around the quad waiting for her. They walked up and down top avenue two or three times hardly saying a word. He was sharing her pain in a silent conversation. Another cadet, returning home early one morning for the funeral of a parent was met by the commissioner just as she was leaving house four. Putting his arm in hers they walked quietly to the main entrance where he left her with a gentle: 'God bless you, Margaret.'

Coutts was equally attentive to the college personnel. One such was the singing company leader at Fulham who worked in the finance department. Needing hospital treatment Connie was surprised when the commissioner arrived to visit her. He chatted with her, to the other patients, offered prayer and handed over a packet of delicious foreign biscuits.

The Couttses became soldiers at Camberwell, a small corps which hosted such training college events as the sessional welcome and farewell weekends, and the famous Thursday night holiness meetings. If the commissioner was away 'specialing' he would ring the corps officer and excuse himself from the Sunday meetings, assuring him of his prayers. Mrs Coutts formed a singing company, and the Couttses collected their district at self-denial time. On Sundays the corps was used as a training centre for cadets and when at home, the commissioner would be present. Then the roles were reversed and he would be preached to by a cadet.

One Sunday that responsibility fell to Cadet Arthur Brown who discovered to his horror that not only was the principal present but he had left his sermon notes at the college. Nevertheless he preached. The following morning there was a handwritten note with the rest of his post:

13.XII.54

Dear Cadet Brown,

I listened with great interest to your address yesterday morning and was blessed by what you said.

Go on to speak with clearness and sincerity—especially sincerity, and God will go on to use you in His service.

God bless you,
Yours sincerely,
F. L. Coutts

Lieut-Commissioner Coutts did not only attend the indoor meetings at Camberwell, but took his bass along to the open-air meetings and took part in the annual carol playing. His ability and desire to communicate the gospel in the open air was now a little different from that first occasion when he was a cadet in Clapton. His philosophy was that wherever the gospel was preached that was holy ground: neither as a corps officer nor as General did he take the open-air ministry lightly. When speaking he would often pull that week's edition of *The War Cry* from his pocket and picking on an article would use it as an introduction: 'On the front page of our *War Cry*—a copy of which you may just have been given. . . .'

Lieutenant and Mrs Norman Bearcroft were welcomed to Camberwell as the new corps officers and, not knowing quite what to expect, the lieutenant arrived at the appointed place for the Sunday morning open-air meeting. By 10.05 there were just four salvationists present: the new officer, the commissioner, the corps sergeant-major in a red tunic, and the colour sergeant. The four stood chatting until the commissioner enquired: 'Are we going to make a start, lieutenant?' 'Yes, commissioner, right away,' came the reply. The lieutenant quickly found a song which he asked the commissioner to lead. 'Is there someone who would lead us in prayer?' asked the lieutenant. Following a few moments silence the commissioner prayed. After leading a song, the new officer stood back in the ring of four and asked if anyone would like to testify. This was apparently something which neither the corps sergeant-major nor the colour sergeant felt able to do and so once more the principal stepped forward to speak and added the invitation to attend the indoor meetings.

This word having been spoken, money was thrown from the six-storey-high flats, some falling amongst the fruit and vegetables from the previous day's market. The commissioner helped to collect this offering. Lieutenant Bearcroft read the Scripture portion after which the principal, smilingly, asked whether the lieutenant would like him to close in prayer as well. 'Yes, please, commissioner', came the reply.

The open-air meeting over, the problem was how to get back to the hall. Seeing Bearcroft's puzzled expression the commissioner again took the initiative: 'We are going to march aren't we?' 'Oh, yes, certainly', was Bearcroft's less than convincing reply.

The corps sergeant major, who had been very silent up to that point, took over: 'We'll march in three's and I'll direct the traffic.' Standing either side of the colour sergeant the two officers marched down the street and out into a busy London road on which the traffic had been brought to a complete halt by the corps sergeant major. To the lieutenant's great amazement, the commissioner started to sing 'If the cross (if the cross) we boldly bear (we boldly bear)'. The colour sergeant did not join in—it was a strange duet and the new officer was never so grateful as when that 'march' arrived back at the hall.

The principal's commitment to the corps and his witness there increased his authority in the eyes of the cadets. They knew that on a Sunday he was as busy proclaiming the gospel as they were. They not only remembered what he said but knew he never asked from them what he did not do himself. His life was a sermon in unspoken salvationism.

Coutts set out deliberately to emphasise the value of the organisation to which the cadets belonged and instilled into them that they could be proud of its achievements.

He did everything in his power to counteract that mentality which says that because something is 'Army' it is therefore inferior to that offered by other churches or religious movements. He believed that the Army was equally as creative and knew how to conduct itself as well as any other group. If it was Army then salvationists must encourage it; support it.

The proper and correct conducting of Salvation Army ceremonies played a large part in Coutts' thinking and was the subject of one of his lectures. Eighteen months before their entry into the college, Cadet and Mrs Ramsay Caffull had been married by the commissioner at Worcester; a ceremony he had agreed to do only if it was a 'uniform wedding'. The commissioner stressed the seriousness of Army ceremonies in general and then called the Caffulls to the platform to help him demonstrate the right procedures for the marriage service because they 'had been through this together before'.

As soon as 'the wedding' was over Mrs Caffull was presented with a doll that until then had been resting in the arms of a woman house officer sitting by the platform. There was now to be a dedication service. This was just too much for the cadets who exploded into laughter. The commissioner became angry, and shouted: 'I will slay you!' The cadets were immediately silenced. The point had been made: ceremonies had to have warmth and dignity.

The commissioner enjoyed a good rapport with his cadets for whom he was an example of Army officership. Occasionally he would take a cadet or two with him 'specialing'. He was to travel to Manchester Star Hall to lead youth councils and decided to take along a house officer, Captain Fleur Booth, and the assistant sergeant-major of the Shepherds Session, Dinsdale Pender. The three travelled together by train from Euston. He joined the officer and cadet on the train, engaged in some brief conversation, took a few minutes to glance at the morning paper, and then dealt with a spate of official correspondence. As the train sped northwards, the principal applied himself to a book review, some writing, and finally reviewed his notes for the weekend. Never a second was wasted.

One winter evening following a carol service in which the children from The Haven had taken part, the sergeant-major of the session was passing the assembly hall in which the lights were still burning. Thinking he would only be turning out the lights, he was taken aback to see the training principal on his knees scraping candle-grease from the beautiful blue carpet. 'Commissioner, you don't have to do that. We'll do it in the morning.' 'Oh, no, my dear sergeant-major,' Coutts replied. 'Nobody is going to clean up my mess.' Together they scraped off the candle grease.

But it was his platform ministry which made the greatest impact on the sessions. He set new, higher standards for the conducting of public worship and the preaching of God's word, standards which the cadets could only dream of attaining. But they did see and hear the best.

However, Coutts' mannerisms still plagued his presentation. Once when leading a corps meeting in Camberwell he paused, his head bowed in characteristic fashion for an even longer period than usual whilst searching for a word. This silence lasted such a long time that an elderly man who was hard of hearing, thinking the sermon was over, stood to his feet and closed the meeting in prayer. If anyone had ever spoken to Coutts about this matter it had not brought about any significant change in his delivery.

Cadets, however, like any other student body, are merciless in that respect. That first Christmas at the college a woman sergeant mimicked him so precisely that she not only scored full marks for entertainment but presented Coutts with a reflection of himself. Thereafter he consciously tried to control his movements whilst speaking. But old habits die hard and there was more than one gesture to copy and several generations of cadets were to rehearse Coutts' gesticulations for fun—only to discover they had unconsciously become part of their own platform manner. When he visited Warrington as General, a friend of the family commented to Mrs Coutts that whilst speaking Frederick 'didn't do so much now with his hands'. 'It was the cadets who cured him of that,' she replied.

At the training college Coutts had to adapt to yet another set of demands with regard to his personal preparation. He now had the same 200 cadets listening to his lectures every week. They were there on Monday mornings for prayers, again for spiritual days and every Thursday evening at Camberwell for the holiness meeting. He had to embody all the principles he wished the cadets to accept. He knew that cadets were hard critics and demanded the best.

Such preparation cost him many extra hours of study. Lieut-Colonel Albert Mingay, the chief side officer for men, had never seen a more industrious man. Coutts was always the first in the office in the morning and often worked late into the evening preparing his platform material. When all the others had gone home, Coutts would put on his old tunic, which was so old and battered that his secretary was ashamed to see him in it, make a pot of tea in his office and get down to work.

This diligence bore much fruit. The college week began with Monday morning prayers in the assembly hall. Even if he had been away 'specialing' he was always present for this meeting. The principal presented series after series of Bible studies in these 'family prayers': Mark's gospel, the epistles of Peter, the letters of John, the Acts of the Apostles, and the continuing adventures of Paul. A cadet would read not more than a dozen verses and then some comments would be offered, no verses or sections were omitted from the books and letters read, and no one wanted to miss them either.

For a spiritual day he would take some great Bible theme or Bible character and develop his thinking over the three meetings. He made profound truths accessible and was blessed with the gift of explanation and teaching. What had begun as a seed-thought and used in the smaller setting of house prayers, later becoming an article for one of the Army papers, then a theme for a spiritual day and finally a chapter in a book.

Coutts was a master craftsman in sermon construction

and could hold a congregation in the palm of his hand. All his efforts were focused on proclaiming the great spiritual truths which moved his own spirit as he preached. The emotion could be heard in his voice. He introduced many new tunes such as 'Salzburg', 'Penlan' and 'Mozart' to the cadets in the spiritual days. Commissioner Coutts was always quiet before and after a meeting, and the quality of the worship he led was such that cadets and officers were reluctant to leave the assembly hall at the close of the day.

The Thursday night holiness meetings at Camberwell which had been instituted twenty-five years previously gave him the opportunity to expound a Bible truth with which he had wrestled for a long time. He delighted again in having a regular congregation, something he had not enjoyed since Clydebank. Some of the Army's finest spirits, including Catherine Baird, were amongst the congregation which came to hear him preach this doctrine. His sermon lasted thirty minutes, starting at 8.30 pm and concluding at 9 pm. One session of cadets was fortunate enough to hear a series of holiness sermons which later became the book *The Call to Holiness*. In the 1955-6 season of holiness meetings more than 200 seekers were registered. One evening a couple knelt at the mercy seat but because of their severe body odour there was a dearth of volunteers to pray with them. Mrs Coutts counselled the woman, the commissioner the man. After the meeting the principal gave money and instructions so that the man had a bed for the night. He then took the woman personally to an Army hostel.

From his youth he had recognised how confusing the whole doctrine of holiness could be and so made the concept of holiness one of the first topics in his articles for *The Warrior*. The confusion amongst young and old regarding this principle of Christian living had not diminished with the years. His starting point in public was simple enough: 'This is a holiness meeting and you would expect me to speak about holiness.' Holiness was for all, not a few. He believed in the necessity of this spiritual experience which he never allowed anyone in private conversation to refer to the Holy Spirit as 'it', and corrected anyone who did so.

His concern was to remove the experience of holiness away from the bizarre, the unusual and the emotional. 'Christlikeness is the best description we have of holiness' he would say and support his definition with the words of the Army Mother who described holiness as 'the simple reception of Christ as an all sufficient Saviour dwelling in my heart and thus cleansing it from all sin.' He was of the opinion that holiness is neither the product of, nor does it proceed from, nor is it necessarily preceded by, some great emotional disturbance. It is a character judgment. 'I define holiness as an experience of God that issues in a life of Christlikeness'; 'Holiness is the unfolding of Christ's own character in the life of the individual believer. . . . He whose example provides the pattern of holy living will, by his grace, provide the power to follow the pattern.'

Coutts taught that this process begins with self surrender, the seeker separating himself unto God and God answering that consecration to his will by filling the seeker's life with his Holy Spirit—that same Spirit who was in Jesus.

Secondly he taught that by that initial step no one is brought into 'final perfection when all character defects are eliminated, when every judgment is sound, when every joy is completed, when all temptations are repulsed with effortless ease. . . . To come to a moment when we feel no need for spiritual improvement would be a moment when we felt no need for God. And that would not be victory but a calamity'.

He wanted to make it clear that living the holy life was not some kind of do-it-yourself spirituality: 'Not a few earnest people still think of holy living in terms of self effort: "I must be kinder"; "I must exercise stricter control of my thoughts". These are most commendable resolves. But perfection is not the fruit of man's best endeavours. Like salvation, it is the gift of God, bestowed in answer to our self-surrender.' This experience, he believed, bestowed victory not immunity from temptation: that it was possible to conquer sin but that the disciple cannot expect to escape what Jesus had to endure.

In his expansion of this teaching he took time and trouble to supply adequate and easily understood definitions of sin and salvation, knowing that if these foundations were not properly laid, the matter of holiness stood no chance of being correctly taught or experienced. How can men speak of purity if they do not understand the meaning of sin?

It was essential for him to restore a note of joy into holiness teaching—it was after all an experience to be enjoyed: 'Holiness is not a cuckoo driving other cherished human joys out of the nest. A man does not love God more by loving his family the less. Holiness is not the foe of human affection. A man has not to cut out his human heart in order to make room for what the familiar line calls "a heart like Thine." Holiness is for the home, for normal people living normal lives.'

He drew his teaching material from the Old and New Testaments, church history, methodism, Army history and the personal experiences of William, Catherine and Bramwell Booth and from Samuel Logan Brengle. It is difficult to assess the impact of his preaching and his writings on this subject upon the Army world. There were few writers who received as much attention as he did on the matter of holiness. In those years the Army published few books, if any, on this topic other than those from Frederick Coutts.

Coutts continued to write regularly for his younger readers in *Vanguard*, occasionally for the weeklies, and contributed the words for three sessional songs whilst training principal: for the Faithful Session when the music was composed by Captain Ray Bowes; the Sword bearers in conjunction with Captain Brindley Boon and the Courageous Session when Captain Dean Goffin wrote the music. But poetry was not his usual medium for expressing his ideas.

The training principal identified himself totally with the cadets even to the point of shocking his hosts. When cadets visited a south coast corps the salvationists were preparing to march away from the sea front. As is often the case, the cadets were placed at the rear of the march. The commissioner moved to the back and took his place behind the cadets' flag. When it was realised that the training principal was not at the front of the march, he was invited to take his place there. 'This is my flag, thank you,' he replied. 'Where it is, I am.'

Men cadets of the Soulwinners Session travelled to Birmingham on campaign. A large number of salvationists assembled for the march. The principal again placed himself at the rear with his men. As the march was about to move off, Cadet Lyndon Taylor took his concertina from its case to play a few choruses. Immediately the commissioner took the bulky case from him and instead of passing it on to someone his 'junior' carried it himself. At the meeting place there was a great deal of rubble which might have proved dangerous for those taking part, so, seeking to avoid an accident, the commissioner singularly cleared the site of dangerous debris.

On campaign in Hull the training principal walked on the pavement, alongside the march, making contact with the general public. He spoke to a man whose wife had just left him with three children to look after. The man attended the Saturday night meeting, returned on Sunday morning and was converted. He became a fine Christian and his children grew up in the corps.

Coutts never forgot his cadets. In later years when reading of their success or special projects he would write a note to congratulate or encourage them. If they were bereaved, they received a message of condolence. When they met he knew their appointments and asked after their children by name. Whilst training principal he would make a point of assembling 'his' lieutenants together around the tea-table if he was visiting a division and if passing through their town or city on a journey, he would arrange to have breakfast with them, or a cup of coffee on the station. He would hand over the leadership of the prayer meeting so he could greet 'one of his own' officers at the back of the hall.

Whilst at the college, Coutts got a great deal of mileage out of his 24-year-old car APH and, on the platform, it became a favourite sermon illustration. It had caught fire one evening as he travelled to a Students' Fellowship meeting to speak to his daughter Margaret whom he asked to come outside because he had something to tell her. He was under farewell orders and was to become territorial commander for the Australia Eastern Territory. Coutts didn't want her to hear it from any one else: that was why he had come. His younger daughter, Elizabeth, now in her middle teens, was very distressed and didn't want to go at all.

In a letter to his secretary dated 4 June 1957, Coutts wrote:

Dear Captain,

The news is out about the farewell. The other appointments involved, including my own, may be published by the end of the week.

Here are four continents all beginning with letter 'A'. Please close your eyes and stick a pin in the correct one.

Africa.   Asia.

America.   Australia.

I heard that Commissioner Grinsted and Colonel Westergaard also have farewell orders.

I hope you are having a good holiday, and with greetings to Gladys.

As ever,
signed F. Coutts

At the time the twelfth session of the International College for Officers was in session. One of the delegates was Major Stan Kingston, divisional commander of the Sydney Central Division which came under Commissioner Coutts' responsibility. The major rang for an appointment to meet his new leader. Upon arrival Coutts offered him a chair and pulled out from his desk drawer a map of Australia which he had been studying. This was the basis of their introductory interview and, with penetrating questions, Coutts pumped the major dry of information about the territory. As always, Coutts, now promoted to commissioner, was extremely thorough in his preparation.

CHAPTER SEVEN

Our sufficiency is of God

Unlike that of thousands of other immigrants entering Australia in 1957, the arrival of Frederick and Bessie Coutts with their teenage daughter Elizabeth, received prominent media coverage.

Following a sea-voyage of several weeks, at nine o'clock on Friday morning 6 September, Sydney Central Railway Station saw 'a great company' of uniformed salvationists, complete with flags and a band, welcoming the territorial commander. That same afternoon tea was taken with his Excellency the Governor-General, Field Marshall Sir William Slim, at Admiralty House overlooking the beautiful Sydney Harbour foreshores. The following evening, at the territory's official public welcome meeting in Sydney Congress Hall, in the presence of civic and church leaders, 'Mrs Coutts proved to be a direct, confident speaker as she declared herself to be entirely dedicated to the task into which she was entering', reported *The War Cry*.

'Though most of us have not previously met Commissioner Coutts, he comes to us as an old friend through his writings,' said Colonel Herbert Wallace, the chief secretary, when introducing the new territorial leader. The commissioner received a standing ovation from the Australian salvationists. *The War Cry* reporter continued: 'He took Paul's example as a guiding principle and demonstrated from Scripture that the apostle, without in any way neglecting church government, would not be deflected from "preaching the gospel in the simplest possible language to the greatest number of people so that the largest possible number might be saved".'

In true Coutts tradition, when introducing himself

through the pages of the Australian *War Cry*, he first of all identified himself with the readers, many of whom were also immigrants but seeking a human utopia. He compared their dreams with the purposes of God and concluded with testimony: 'If, however, a new arrival reaches these shores with a faith in God and the love of God shed abroad in his heart, then he is the kind of immigrant who may rightly be welcomed even by those who may not share his experience. . . . A faith in God means that a man is not so credulous as to suppose that his unaided efforts can move the mountains which bar the way to a more perfect society, but that with God is the power to bring to pass a Kingdom in which sin will have lost its sting and the grave its victory.

'To this last company I belong . . . simply as one who believes in the Christian way, and believes in it so implicitly that he tries to shape his personal life upon its pattern through knowing its power in his own heart. To all who share this faith—within and without The Salvation Army—I give my hand and they will grip it without my asking. To those who do not share this faith I offer my hand as well, for nothing would please me better and profit you more than to be led to its author—Jesus Christ, the Saviour of men.'

This was yet another world for the Couttses. Known as 'excitement city', Sydney is the oldest, largest and most colourful city in the country. Whilst it has its poorer areas, the city is also modern and sophisticated. There was little comparison with Red Tiles or the depressing tenement buildings around Camberwell Green. Neither could this new responsibility be compared to the compact, small world of the training college where everything and everyone was near to hand. Sydney didn't have London smog; there was room to breathe, to be free, to relax in a beautifully warm climate more suited to leisure than to work. The Australian mentality was so different from anything he had ever met before: the drive to be out of doors, looking for adventure or recreation, and that overriding compulsion to enjoy life on the beach. Instead of speaking about Birmingham or Warrington, they now spoke of Gympie, Toowong, Woolloongabba and Boonah.

Their new home at 5 River Street, Blakehurst, in a charming residential suburb on the southern side of Sydney, overlooking a river, was not far from Botany Bay. Mrs Coutts would have loved to have glassed-in the back of the house so that she could enjoy the sunshine, and sew or paint there. But the commissioner would not agree to it because he thought it would cost too much and other officers had less.

If the contrast in life-style constituted a cultural shock for the Couttses, then it was no less a shock for the territory. Coutts followed Commissioner Edgar Grinsted and their personalities were in direct contrast. Grinsted was larger than life, had flair, was flamboyant and demonstrative. He could excite and enthuse his hearers. For three years, with seemingly untiring vitality, Grinsted had blazed a path across the territory. Coutts did not project himself; it was noticed that the new commissioner didn't often clap his hands to the congregational singing, and didn't seem to share the Australian's enthusiasm for drum-beating and flag waving. He was reserved and had little small talk. However they soon learned that Commissioner Coutts could inspire by what he said rather than the manner in which it was spoken.

Upon taking office, the first thing he did was to pay tribute to the work of his predecessor; something he did in all his appointments. He was never in competition with the man he followed; never finding it necessary to demolish his predecessor's work in order to allow his own to be seen more clearly.

Just as when a boy, Coutts was again challenged to learn new slang, new passwords and a new dialect if he was to survive. Coutts set about that task with enthusiasm. He listened to the radio programme 'English for New Australians' which he thought was mainly for the benefit of non-English speaking immigrants; but he had reason to think again. Once when Coutts visited an officer's family the parents became increasingly uneasy at their son's use of slang in front of the territorial commander, but rather than being embarrassed by the new words,

Coutts, his eyes twinkling with private humour, seemed to be pushing the lad to say more. In bandsman's councils the next day, to the great delight of his young teacher, the commissioner used some of the words he had learned. And yet again the experience was translated into a principle: the more he thought about the open-air meeting, the more certain he became that there should be 'a course in non-Christian language for Christians'.

Even though he tried to identify himself with the Australians, he often delighted his listeners with stories against himself and his 'Pommie' extraction. And he kept his links with England: writing for his faithful readers in *Vanguard* about current issues such as war and the atom bomb, and his new life in Australia. His former editorial colleagues also kept in touch—especially at Christmas when sixteen of them signed a greeting composed by Bernard Watson:

> A band of fellow pilgrims, who remember you with affection and who take pride in having worked with you, send this token of sincere friendship. As you are of the Apostolate of Poverty, there is no need for us to apologise for inability to give gold, silver or precious stones. . . . We have confidence you will be unspoilt by applause, wary of adulation, shy as of yore, with enough proper pride to prevent your ever being other than the man we knew.

In the late 1950s, The Salvation Army in Australia was still reflecting its English heritage. An Australian Salvation Army identity was just emerging and apparently not everyone was happy with another Englishman as leader. One officer at the Newcastle divisional welcome offered the following in his speech: 'Commissioner, we see that most of our leaders that come from England wear very high collars on their tunics.' Shaking his head from side to side he asked: 'Is that so you can only say "no" and not "yes"?'

'I can still say "yes", even if it means undoing my collar,' came the commissioner's reply.

At territorial headquarters Coutts began a new style of

management, being the first commissioner to leave his desk and go to the respective employee or officer to ask for what he wanted. He did not expect them always to come to him. He had a meticulous eye for detail and, though delegating, would interest himself in all aspects of any project which came before him. He didn't just accept people's word for things but checked the facts himself. He faced up to difficulties and investigated problems thoroughly to get at the truth.

No one left his office in any doubt as to what the decision was, no was no, and yes was yes, and they knew that they could not change his mind afterwards either. He gave people time and, as far as he was able, explained the why and wherefore of their appointment or the reasons for the decision which had been taken. If necessary, or if he thought it best, in matters of administration or of 'justice', he was prepared to be the misunderstood party. Because of these factors and because he could say 'no' in such a gracious manner, the anger some felt or the disappointment they bore when not getting what they had set their hearts upon, was a little easier to cope with. He would stand by his officers, disciplining them if necessary, but he never steam-rollered anyone in order to get his own way.

Coutts' concern for his officers was clearly manifest. One evening he heard that an officer in a distant corps had resigned. That night he boarded a plane, transferred on to a train in the middle of the trip, and next morning arrived at the officer's quarters to pray with him. It was the same spirit he had displayed as a lieutenant all those years ago in the north of England. He intervened in matters of farewells if he thought that the children's education was at risk. When word came to him that a woman officer had formed a friendship with a non-salvationist, he called her to his office and suggested that they keep it quiet until she had made a definite decision. He did not wish to jeopardise the possibility of her remaining an officer by taking any official action too soon.

In 1935 he had left corps work and twenty-two years later he was a territorial commander without having had the experience of being a divisional commander, field secretary or chief secretary. As the top man he now had to make decisions regarding all aspects of a diverse administration, including the social services of which he had no managerial experience. In that sense he was unprepared and inexperienced for such an appointment; his skills and abilities lay in communication not in Salvation Army management. Commissioner Harry Warren, who served Coutts as field secretary and later as chief secretary, wrote: 'If ever Frederick Coutts was at a disadvantage in his first and only territorial command, his experience and observations elsewhere made him a fast learner in the Australian scene.'

In the various committees essential to the smooth running of a territory Coutts listened intently to all that was said, especially to advice. He would make a careful mental note of every observation, follow up leads, courteously ask questions and, when necessary, 'play the innocent' before coming to an unhurried decision. He wouldn't allow decisions to be made without due thought and consideration. When trying to get an argument straight, or tackle an unclear question his introduction would be: 'Yes . . . hum . . . that is to say, no.' Or when scanning an agenda: 'Let us take the easy ones first' in order to clear the table for the major issues. Even when he felt strongly about a matter, he always remained courteous; his natural reserve and economy of words giving greater weight to his opinions. He never generalised and was non-committal in the absence of evidence.

All his committee meetings began on a sound spiritual basis. The commissioner himself made this clear: 'I have never attended any council or conference whether concerned with finance—for example, in the shape of budget proposals or balance sheets—or with appointments—whether these have had to do with corps officers or territorial commanders—or the application or amendment of regulations, without the business of the day being prefaced by some such prayer as: "Give thy guidance in all these things which concern thy Kingdom." This does not, I repeat, confer immunity from errors of judgment at any level, but he would be a doubting Thomas indeed who did not believe that the Holy Spirit is pleased to answer, as seemeth him good, the very kind of prayer which he has bidden us offer.'

It was perhaps for that reason that he was never in a hurry when appointing officers: he sought guidance. The facts, the details and the timing were all important. Personal integrity was as important to him as leadership ability. Where possible, he tried to make sure that people received some kind of training for the job they would be taking over and were as far as possible, ready to accept that responsibility. But he had received no training for his appointment and did not pretend otherwise. He was always prepared to ask for help and information. When carrying out his first divisional inspection he said to the divisional commander: 'Well, major, I must confess that I shall have to rely on your help in this responsibility: I have never before had to carry out such an inspection.'

Because he was not always directive, those who did not wish to co-operate thought they could stone-wall him. They didn't say they wouldn't help, but never got round to doing things as asked. But Coutts wore such people down. He didn't become angry, didn't bang his fist on the table: he telephoned and asked if they had remembered it; or he would go down to their office and ask for it. There was an iron fist in a velvet glove. Those imagining him to be weak had misunderstood his gentlemanly style. He didn't forget anything.

There were those who felt his style was too conservative, they were disappointed that he didn't show more daring. Only after much hesitation did he eventually appoint a stewardship secretary and establish a stewardship programme. He was ever cautious, reluctant in the question of using non-salvationist professional services. Australia Eastern was after all a growing territory with opportunities.

He may not have been an entrepreneur, but there was a persistent drive towards an objective. In officers' councils in May 1958, following the annual congress in

Sydney, Coutts challenged his officers as to the future goals for the territory. Large posters summarised the statistical history of the territory and population increases. The Army's relative progress was indicated.

'After a consideration of these figures it was agreed that the territorial goal should be at least the maintenance of an equal Salvation Army strength against the steadily rising population,' reported *The War Cry*. 'Detailed study was given to the soul-saving possibilities of broadcasting, of work among the young people, through the home league, in social institutions and by the personal life and example of each officer.'

The commissioner followed the example of his predecessor and called for experienced officers to offer to spend five years in difficult appointments. Volunteers presented themselves privately and the strategy succeeded.

Coutts had the policy of keeping in close contact with his divisional commanders, suggesting ideas and projects. He was always especially interested in the training college and was most attentive to the curriculum. When the cadets held their field days in Sydney they were marathon events. And the commissioner was there right from the first open-air meeting in the morning through to the evening meeting which he conducted.

One of his concerns about the Army in general was the way in which some salvationists spoke about the movement: 'We could well manifest a tender concern for the Army. She is the mother of us all, and no one runs down his mother in public. She doubtless has her idiosyncracies and her faults, but to these one does not draw public attention, rather continuing to entreat her privately as a son.'

A second source of unrest was for him the way in which some officers spoke about their colleagues. He wanted that no one go beyond the strict bounds of 'the truth, the whole truth, and nothing but the truth'. And even when what was said was true, it had to be spoken in love. 'Truth spoken in anger, or bitterness, or in irritation is truth distorted. It could even be truth so twisted as to become untruth. But for truth to retain its pure colouring it must be the truth spoken in love.'

A further matter which he constantly brought to the attention of officers and cadets alike, was that of letter writing. A letter should be written so carefully and neatly that it is asking to be read, was his principle. He insisted that letters were written to be answered, and answered courteously. Hard things can be said softly in a conversation, the sting may be removed by a caring attitude, but a letter is different—the receiver reads it cold and sees only the words. Coutts explained that a letter was 'not a device by which I can tell a man something which I would not dare to say to his face. And when I write a letter, and have to say even the most difficult truths in it, it must be the kind of document that I would not be ashamed of having placed before me again: "Look, you wrote that."

'There is a way of letting off steam by letter. It is to sit down before one's typewriter, and really let oneself go. Don't post it that night. Wait until next morning—and then tear it up. . . . Never write a long letter if a shorter one will do. Remember, the longer the letter you write—especially if it is an argumentative one—the more room you give to the receiver to find a flaw, to pick some hole, especially if he is out to evade your main point.'

Upon receiving a letter about an article he had written, there was the danger that a lengthy and complicated theological correspondence would begin. To avoid this his reply was simply:

Dear Friend,
I am grateful for your letter, which I have read with care, regarding the Christmas article. My own position is that of the orthodox believer who holds that there is one God known as Father, Son and Holy Spirit. More than this I cannot say. May His blessing and guidance continue to be yours.

It was his aim to visit every corps in the territory and to lead a meeting there. On one tour he travelled 5,000 miles. Even though they knew that the commissioner was

111

coming, it was a surprise for the soldiers to see him sometimes waiting at the door, giving out the song books and greeting everyone individually as they entered the hall. He made a deep impression on soldiers and officers alike, one reason being that he never demanded his place. When telephoning an officer it was simply: 'Coutts here, major.' In the billets he would take the tea-towel and dry the dishes. He became angry only when other people were not given their proper place.

Again his popular appeal was to the young who sought him out for advice on moral and religious issues. He was at ease with them, respected their views, and won their friendship. His public speaking let the mature salvationist know that here was a leader who was in touch with the real world in which he lived. He knew what they were experiencing because he took the trouble to find out. He became a hero whose presence in the movement made others proud to remain in the ranks: if Coutts could remain, then they could stay as well. His example fired allegiance.

In the spring of 1960 the Randwick Municipal Council refused the Army permission to build a hall and community service centre on a recently acquired site in Boyce Road, Maroubra. Headed by the national flag and the flag of The Salvation Army, Commissioner and Mrs Coutts and more than 200 salvationists marched through the Maroubra Junction Shopping Centre in Sydney to protest the decision. There were songs, banners and boards with slogans, music and speeches. It became a public debate with the Mayor of Randwick presenting the council's point of view and the commissioner the views of the Army.

Three years later an advertisement appeared in *The War Cry* inviting people to attend a meeting of thanksgiving for the rescinding of the council's 1960 decision and for which invitations had been sent out to the mayor and councillors of the borough.

As the active wife of the territorial commander Mrs Coutts revelled in this new role: all the characteristics of her corps officer life-style were seen again. Along with her other responsibilities, Mrs Coutts committed herself again to the work of the Students' Fellowship which met at one of the social centres in the heart of Sydney. The fellowship was only as successful as it was because of her initiative and interest. It was an exciting group to belong to and Mrs Coutts kept her husband primed with their thoughts.

Within the territory there was an urgent need to spend a great deal of money up-dating social service centres and to remodernise corps halls: 'The rapid economic growth of our commonwealth must be matched by increasing provision for the moral and spiritual needs of our people. . . . I shall appeal for money on the ground that an investment of this kind will pay dividends in character and righteousness which cannot be valued on any stock exchange,' said Coutts. And in 1960 the territory opened at least one new Army building every month.

Though he is not often thought of in terms of being an evangelist, Frederick Coutts deserves that description. What is striking is that whatever appointment he held, his desire to communicate the gospel and to address the man in the street in an intelligent and interesting manner was his prime concern. His Bible notes for an open-air talk were as carefully prepared as any word he ever spoke in an indoor meeting. He took the same amount of trouble for the sinner being called to repentance as for the saint being called to live the life of holiness.

As the territorial commander he never missed the chance to attend the open-air meeting and to testify if the opportunity was given. His early arrival at the place where the meeting was to be held and his witness there was an example to officer and soldier alike. He stated his reasons why in an article published in 1959 after he had led the very first televised open-air meeting in the Australia Eastern Territory:

If anyone was to ask me why The Salvation Army is not content to hold its meetings indoors in its own buildings, but, in summer and winter alike, is to be found in the open air, I would give two main reasons.

113

Neither has anything to with the Army as such, but everything to do with the nature and meaning of the Christian religion.

The first is that in taking our stand out of doors in this fashion we are declaring that the Christian gospel is not for the sole benefit of those who are in the habit of regularly attending a place of worship, but has something to say for the good of all men everywhere. . . . The second reason is that if the gospel can mean so much to all men, then it must be proclaimed where men and women are, so that at least they may know what they are accepting or rejecting. No human decision matters so much as this one.

It was perhaps this fire within him to spread the good news of the gospel which also determined his attitude towards broadcasting: he realised that thousands would be able to hear the gospel via the radio and television who might never darken the doors of a church. He wanted the Army to be involved. Amongst the first Army broadcasts in the territory were those live from Sydney Congress Hall. Later, pre-recorded meetings reached listeners 4,000 miles away.

Coutts was a master of this medium. Salvationists in Australia heard a Coutts which no other territory ever did. His broadcasts in the series entitled, 'Plain Christianity', are classics. They prove how a deep spirituality can be successfully communicated through modern words to a modern world. In these broadcasts he had just the right word for each moment—even to introducing the songster brigade: 'Our territorial singers will further remind us of the presence of the living Lord in our midst, in your home, in our world, as they now sing "In the secret of Thy presence".' He never employed cheap, easy Christian clichés. He was succeeding in his aim not to allow the burdens of administration to prevent him preaching the gospel in 'the simplest possible language to the greatest number of people so that the largest possible number might be saved.' Neither before nor again was he afforded the opportunity to use the medium of radio and television so effectively.

114

If his preaching had set the Australian salvationist back on his heels, his ability to communicate was making its impact on other Christians, too. There was a growing number of invitations for him to preach in their churches and lecture in their theological colleges. Wherever he went in his capacity as territorial leader, there was a policy to invite civic and church leaders to be present. He wanted to see the Army taking its rightful place in the life and witness of the Church. This was a very precious theme in his thinking. He believed with all his heart that the Army need not be ashamed of its theology, nor its practices nor consider itself to be in any way, shape or form, a second-class body of Christians.

For this reason the Army accepted its responsibilities in various councils of churches. Said Coutts: 'We would be denying our place if we did not take our place. I understand our Founder's severance from the churches—with a small 'c'—but in doing so he did not sever himself from the Church—with a capital 'C'. If we fail to make that distinctive contribution to the life of the Church which the Army alone can make, we are doing a disservice to him who is Lord of the Church and by whose grace we are members of the Church.'

Coutts claimed that salvationists were not outsiders. 'As we have freely received from our fellow believers in the historic churches, we are required freely to give. So we offer three distinctive contributions to the life of the Church as a whole:

(a) The witness of a disciplined Army.
(b) The example of dedicated youth.
(c) The testimony of redeeming lives.'

The qualification for belonging to the Church was for Coutts also simple enough: 'Whoever acknowledges Jesus as Saviour belongs to the Church; whom Christ has accepted cannot be disenfranchised.' The Army does all the things a church does: 'We worship, we teach, praise, shepherd our people and proclaim the gospel.'

This thinking was a complete cycle of events so far as Salvation Army history was concerned and Coutts had certainly experienced much of that change. At the start William Booth had tried to link up his converts with the established churches but the attempt had failed. In 1882 arrangements had even been made for salvationists who wished to, to receive the sacraments from the hands of anglican priests, but the plan was sufficiently unacceptable to certain parties within the churches to make it unworkable. The *Church Times* protested. The result was that·The Salvation Army remained separate from the churches, with all the inevitable consequences. There was nothing in writing: it was 'an atmosphere', 'an attitude', that the Army did not actively promote a working together with other churches.

In his appraisal of this matter Coutts noted that a more united approach to the churches was once seen as 'anathema' and later he softened this term to 'frowned upon'. But Coutts had always done his best to promote a working together with all churches, even as a corps officer. He sought to be on good terms with all churches and hostile to none. And for this as with all other aspects of Salvation Army life he went back to the Bible and to the movement's history.

He took comfort from the words of General Bramwell Booth recorded in *Echoes and memories*: 'There is one Church. . . . Of this, the great Church of the living God, we claim, and have ever claimed, that we of The Salvation Army are an integral part and element—a living fruit-bearing branch of the True Vine. . . . We believe then that our Lord Jesus Christ has called us into his Church of the redeemed, that our call has not been by man or the will of man, but by the Holy Spirit of God. . . .'

Coutts was also influenced in these matters by Commissioner A. G. Cunningham who represented the Army at the founding of the World Council of Churches, in 1948, a body which accorded with his philosophy that all men are brothers. But he was also totally aware of the things which prevented fuller unity: 'There remains a large question mark against administrative union. Rite and sacrament still sadly divide. They have long done so. Men have argued endlessly about the nature of their observance, and have almost excommunicated one another because of their differences. But salvation—this personal acceptance of Jesus as Saviour, this basic requirement—this surely unites us all. There is nothing in this basic experience to set believers at variance with one another. We gather around the same Cross. We cast ourselves believingly upon the same Saviour.'

He believed that the ordination of women would have to come in the life of the Church and was very sad when hearing of single women officers who were approached by clergy to perform some kind of practical work, but who were not given their right of place in a church service or civic function. But such a devotee of Catherine Booth could not think otherwise. When arguing the case for women being active as ministers Coutts began by placing the role of women in its historical, social and Church history contexts. He examined prejudices and placed the matter in the setting of the New Testament and Salvation Army history. These conclusions he called 'The benefits of this practice':

1. A healthy corporate atmosphere in which men and women recognise together the complementary parts which each can play in the Christian cause. Any sense of superiority or fear of inferiority disappears. 'Gone is the distinction' as St Paul said in his letter to the Galatians (3:28) 'between male and female'.
2. A wider outreach. We of The Salvation Army would lose half our effective officer strength if our women officers were disbarred from following the vocation to which they sincerely feel that God has called them.
3. A common dedication. That wretched thing called the sex war vanishes when men and women share in a common effort—especially this noblest effort of all, the spread of the Christian gospel.

His stand regarding the non-use of the sacraments was not just a blind acceptance of a tradition: it was a studied point of view. Uncharacteristically he had a rather expensive linen and cardboard tile which had in the top left hand corner, in blue stencilled capitals,

SACRAMENTS. Inside, amongst the twenty-eight items was a typed copy of an article which had appeared in *Review of the Churches* in April 1895 entitled 'Salvation Army problems—Important pronouncements by the General'. Whilst on a sea voyage, General William Booth had given an interview to Sir Henry Lunn in which the Founder had outlined the Army's position on the sacraments. There was a book belonging to Theo H. Kitching, published in 1882, written by an anglican vicar asking the question through its title: 'The two sacraments, so called, are they institutions of Christ?'

Further there was a book of 230 pages of scholarly essays from distinguished writers entitled *Sacraments: their psychology and history*; booklets and pamphlets from the Society of Friends; various articles, one of twenty-three and another of eighteen pages typed out because the days of photocopying had not yet arrived.

For many years it was the Army's policy not only to abstain from taking the sacraments but also from any public discussion of the issue. It is perhaps for this reason that so many wild stories and misunderstandings sprang up amongst salvationists concerning the non-use of the sacraments. Fortunately Coutts had not pursued the rule of silence but had followed his intellect and when a storm broke on this issue with the Australian Council of Churches, Coutts could give reasons for the Army's position.

When being interviewed or when lecturing about these matters he would say very gently and in a non-campaigning spirit that he did not expect or ask others 'to agree with us'. Painstakingly he would say that the Army was not in opposition to the sacraments and that these symbols could be a means of grace to those who wished to observe them. If he stressed that the Army was not against the sacraments, he also stressed that the movement was not theologically careless in this matter nor did it possess a kind of slap-happy evangelism which thinks it to be of no consequence. 'It is very hard for the most sympathetic outsider to understand the Army's position on this matter,' he admitted but felt that The

Salvation Army, along with the Society of Friends, had a duty to testify to other churches that neither physical elements nor the need for another person to act as an intermediary were necessary to receive grace. He was always careful not to give the impression that the sacraments were something which the Army would like to see abolished, but was concerned when form seemed to be more important than the reality. 'Our people do receive grace, and if they were lacking in any grace then we would be required to look at the matter again.'

But working with the churches had more than just theological implications; there were sometimes gentleman's agreements about evangelism in missionary fields which were to have repercussions later. That had been the case at the turn of the century when various protestant churches had agreed a policy with regard to evangelising the people of New Guinea, later Papua New Guinea. Geographically Papua New Guinea is (after Australia) the world's largest island possessing some of the world's most inhospitable terrain. Because the nation's life-style was so primitive, the churches approached William Booth when he visited Australia in the early 1900s, and asked him not to start any work there. They were anxious about the confusion it would cause the native population. There was nothing signed, but he agreed.

By 1938 the unwritten agreement was breaking down and a survey was carried out to see if The Salvation Army in Australia could begin some kind of work there. However there were no officers available and because war broke out in 1939, nothing came of it. After the war the returning Australian soldiers had reason to be grateful to their native stretcher-bearers who had earned themselves the respectful and legendary nick-name of 'Fuzzy-wuzzy-angels'.

The returning veterans put pressure on the Army to do something for the Papuans and so another survey was carried out. In August 1956, under the leadership of Senior-Major Keith Baker, and ten weeks later Lieutenant Ian Cutmore, Army work was begun in New Guinea.

Although enormously well received by those administering the island which was still technically governed by Australia, the salvationists were not always warmly received by the other missions already there. Commissioner Grinsted who had given the green light for the project received farewell orders so that the resulting ill-will caused by the New Guinea enterprise came to rest on the desk of his successor. Some felt that the Army had broken its word. Coutts had to walk a diplomatic tightrope.

But Coutts could not have supported this project any better if it had been his own idea. Though he did not stimulate any particular expansion of the work, he selected most carefully the officers to be sent to the new field. Corps, medical, social and educational work expanded in Papua, and national cadets were also trained on the island. He was impressed by the country and its potential, he understood the struggles, and followed all developments very closely. He took a personal interest in what was happening, visiting the island more than six times.

When visitors were few and far between, the Couttses arrived on the island to see for themselves what was happening. They stayed several days with a New Zealand nurse, Captain Dorothy Elphick, and an Australian nurse, Lieutenant Beulah Harris. The quarters in the Eastern Highlands were made of bamboo; there was a water shortage and the commissioner received an electric jug full of water with which he could do as he pleased—but that was his ration, not one drop, for whatever reason, could be added. There were only two or three hours electricity per day.

In the crowded streets of Port Moresby, Saturday night open-air meetings were held in front of a hotel. The warm tropical nights with the noise in the streets and from the bars made for boisterous occasions. Those who stopped to listen were the nationals who hardly understood any English, and the whites who could understand were not at all interested. One such Saturday night, Commissioner Coutts took the opportunity to speak: the whites were arrested firstly by the authority he projected and later by what he was saying. He controlled the crowd as if it was a congregation listening to a holiness address in a Salvation Army hall. When he spoke there was an aura about him.

Coutts did everything possible to build a strong bridge between the salvationists in Australia and the native people of New Guinea, often arranging for groups of salvationists to be brought across for congress meetings.

Those who drove Coutts have memories of hours of excruciating silence; the chauffeurs eventually giving up all attempts at conversation. Even when it was just himself and one another, there was, more often than not, nothing to say. But when it mattered he did have something to say because he read: on train and air journeys he was absorbed in his reading. He read rapidly, carrying an endless supply of books in his bag. Whilst reading, Coutts would sigh, or chuckle quietly to himself, pencil in a note and then invite discussion with his companion by asking: 'What do you think of this?' Only then was it time to talk.

Coutts was now able to expand his ministry of teaching with regard to the doctrine of holiness in a different way from that used at the International Training College. He instigated the Brengle institutes in the territory, handling himself such topics as: 'A right conception of sin'; 'The work of grace in the man of God'; 'The history of holiness'; 'The doctrine of holiness in the song book'; 'The man of God and the life of holiness' and 'Holiness in Army life and letters'. He wanted to rid the doctrine of any association with sanctimoniousness—telling of the convert who was not hard to get on with until he became 'sanctified'.

He did not wish the blessing of holiness to be identified with those who, thinking they had achieved a certain level of holiness, sat in terrible judgment upon others. He also made it plain that holiness is not the enemy of natural desires and the basic instincts of life which are to be enjoyed. 'Must we only weep and not laugh in His presence? Is it godly to mourn and ungodly to rejoice?' he asked his congregations. 'I have yet to fulfil the desire of years and speak one Sunday morning about the marriage of holiness and humour,' he wrote in 1960. 'What God hath joined we have sadly put asunder.'

'My teaching concerning the experience of holiness must be intelligible and practical. That is to say, it must be adapted to the needs of the man who has his living to earn in a fiercely competitive world, and to the mother who carries the responsibility of a growing family; to the young man or woman concerned with business or academic studies or living in an environment where Christian truth is dismissed—if not often derided—as irrelevant.' So he prepared relevant talks for youth councils about holiness at school; holiness in the home; holiness and social activities'.

Frederick Coutts had certainly been blessed with the gifts of teaching and preaching.

CHAPTER EIGHT

As one having authority

Frederick Coutts had made a study of preaching and just as any other creative spirit closely examines the work of others in his field, especially those who are better than he, Coutts had done that with the art of exposition. He read books of sermons and was a regular reader of the *Expository Times*. He listened, read and learned from others how best he could improve his own talent. When on honeymoon he and his wife had queued to lilsten to a great preacher. Right through his life he concentrated on this art, so spoke as one having authority.

He was concerned that much Salvation Army activity was not providing practical and actual Christian guidance to the soldier about how he ought to live. Though salvationists may be very busy in the corps, it concerned him that the actual time they were taught from the word of God was 'marginal'. Because of this he regarded the time that people came together for worship to be precious and would not waste a moment of it: 'Say that, on an average, our people attend three indoor meetings a week—a total of not more than four hours, which is just over two per cent of a weekly total of 168 hours . . . and there are some of our people who hear the word of God and share in prayer only when they attend a meeting. I do not reproach them, much less condemn them, but how to help them? To this end, how can I make the best use of that fragment of their time when they are at one of my meetings?

'Our people need instruction in the none too easy art of Christian living if they are to stand against the open attack of hostile ideologies as well as the creeping paralysis of indifference. All the intricate administrative machinery of the Army will become little more than a mass of wheels rotating at speed unless our people who man the front line in factory, mill, mine and shop are adequately instructed in their most holy faith. To instruct is our responsibility. If our soldiery are ill-equipped mentally as well as spiritually, the most brilliant staff work will not save us.'

He knew that a speaker is not automatically the focus of attention: people have their worries and concerns which distract them. It can happen that there is some unhappiness or tension in the salvationist family when they were hurriedly preparing to go to the hall. Others attend only because of parental pressure, their interests lying far from the world of the Spirit. So his plea was for relevant worship with a Salvation Army character and the distinct style of a praise, holiness or salvation meeting, in order to distinguish it from a church service. He wrote:

Every Army meeting is a living thing which can flourish or die—and sometimes it is I, the leader, who can wound it mortally. It is because an Army meeting is a living thing that a good Army meeting can reach such heights. The ladder we raise can reach the heavens so that upon it, as with Jacob's ladder, angels can descend and ascend to the blessing of the congregation. But at other times it does not rise six inches from the ground, chained down by my waffling and unnecessary off-the-cuff remarks. Because the less well I am prepared, the more verbose I am likely to be. . . . For if I do not know where I am going, neither will the congregation. I am to lead my people to the throne of grace. But no casual approach on my part will get me within miles of the throne of grace.

He urged simplicity; what did it matter if others more learned thought the material was elementary? 'Unless I am understood by my congregation I am wasting my time.' His advice was to make it plain, if necessary with words of one syllable. Introducing his text, 1 Timothy 4:12 he began: 'Here then it is. Less than a dozen words from the Bible. Nine of them words of a single syllable. Always the best kind of words to use in public speaking. "Let no man despise thy youth; but be thou an example. . . ." There is no possible room for misunderstanding.'

When leading a meeting, his own comments were minimal. In response to a word of welcome that might have stolen valuable time, he would reply: 'We are grateful to you, major, for your kind words. I pray, as we all pray, that this meeting will be a means of grace to everyone who is present.' Whether it was the collection, or the songster brigade, the introduction was often not more than a sentence.

For him there was no less important or more important meeting: every meeting was just as vital as the other, demanding the most detailed and careful preparation of heart and mind. The final chorus was as important as the opening verse. 'Whence comes this idea that unless I am standing before the microphone facing a crowded Royal Albert Hall then I need not bother to prepare? An audience of 100 is not ten times more important than one of ten. . . . Immortal issues are at stake as much for six as 600. . . . He that is unfaithful in little may also be unfaithful in much.'

Coutts was a great believer in the principle that worship is the work of people and it cannot be a proper Salvation Army meeting if the officer does everything. He sought the maximum participation of those present. He encouraged people to pray and to testify. Early in his stay as a corps officer, he devoted three consecutive Sundays' meetings to the matter of prayer: private prayer, family prayer and public prayer. When he came to the third meeting about the use and manner of public prayer he pointed the congregation to the song book in which those comrades who had difficulty in finding the right words to say could find assistance in the words of a song.

It was not because he did not know how to pray that the opportunity was given for others to speak to God on behalf of the congregation, he said. Neither was it because he was too lazy or didn't want to lead the congregation in prayer. He could do it all from A to Z, but experience had taught him that in most meetings there is someone who wants to pray, either for himself, someone in his family or the corps. To the more shy he would gently ask, 'Come on, pray now, Jim'. Because he knew that if Jim got the victory this time, Sue would the next. 'We should ever remember that a prayer meeting is a meeting where people pray. Many officers regret the lack of spontaneous, voluntary prayer in some corps. The remedy is not to make do without prayer and fill up with choruses, nor to call on particular comrades to pray. Let the need be ventilated in the band spiritual meeting, the corps cadet class, the soldiers' meeting, and let our people be told why it is that prayer in our meetings is not—as in many other places of worship—the duty of one man.'

Coutts applied the same principle to the testimony period which he believed to be an essential part of salvationist worship. Preaching and testimony go hand in hand, he maintained. Testimony was to attract people to the gospel and persuade them to listen to it. It provided a living example of the truth which is being proclaimed. Testimony confirms the truths preached. But in these matters, when people were reluctant to speak or pray, he was not judgmental for he had suffered deep humiliation in these matters himself when a teenager.

He was anxious to see the same kind of planning by meeting leaders as by musicians who knew in advance what they would sing or play and who prepared themselves for that event. Why it seldom happened that salvationists were asked, for instance, a week in advance to prepare a testimony, for either an indoor or outdoor meeting, remained a puzzle to him. This kind of notice to speak was necessary because testifying puts people on the spot. Spiritual success and failure come to light. People must not be put in a position of wasting the congregation's time because they have not had the chance to prepare properly.

'The worth of my testimony depends upon my personal credibility,' he said. 'I have to begin—and end—with what I can say for myself. What I say must be supported by what I am. . . . We ourselves must stand where we would have others come. . . . If we are not near the cross, we have

no place to which to invite the weary and heavy laden
. . . personal experience is either an asset or a liability.
I must not gild the lily. I must neither overstate nor
understate the facts of my personal experience.'

Though he promoted honest testimony in which people
were encouraged to speak in the first person singular, in
his preaching the word 'I' hardly ever appeared. When
he did speak about himself it was generally via a reference
to an unknown third party. It was essential that the
speaker never got in the way of the message with too
many 'I's. The work of the preacher is not to proclaim
his own ideas and opinions. However correct they may
be, they do not count, was his conclusion.

The reading of the Bible portion, which could also be
presented by someone other than the officer, was also
intended to be a means of grace for the congregation: to
be read slowly, thoroughly rehearsed and plainly heard.
Regarding modern translations, his argument was not that
the chosen translation be that which the preacher
preferred but that which the people find most helpful.

Neither did he address the congregation as 'you' nor
speak of 'your band'. He spoke always of 'our songster
brigade', 'our commanding officer', 'our corps'. When he
used 'we' or 'my' he really meant 'us'. He identified
himself completely with his listeners and the message;
Coutts was angry when a speaker distanced himself from
the congregation. Of one occasion he wrote:

At a certain series of youth councils it was urged that
there should be more youth participation. Less
prominence to bald heads and gold braid and more of
youth speaking to youth. Fine! Let the lads and girls
themselves handle the matter—for example—of
candidates—and then I listened to the lad who engaged
in prayer on this very point. 'Lord, if there are those
here whom you call, may they hear your voice and obey
your will.' Never 'may we hear your voice and obey
your will'. By the use of the third person plural the lad
neatly contracted out of the possibility that God might
be speaking to him. It was they, not we or I, to whom
God should speak.

'Too often we divide the Army into "they" and "we" . . . in reality, however, the Army is "us",' Coutts wrote in a corps magazine. He possibly adopted this attitude having been deeply affected by a small but significant custom followed by the Army Mother: her use of the pronoun 'we' in her addresses. In one of his talks to officers, Coutts records that when speaking to the outcast or socially deprived, Catherine Booth 'would use some such phrase as: "We, who stand in need of God's forgiveness" or "We, whose only hope is in his grace". Always "we", identifying herself with her hearers as being, with them, in need of the forgiving love of God. But not only in my preaching but in my practice as well, I must identify myself with those in my care.'

Coutts had spent most of his officership preaching in a different corps each Sunday, but knew that the burden was really with the corps officer who faced the same congregation week in and week out, with all the attendant difficulties which drive men to all kinds of solutions including ministers' manuals, that is, books containing ready-made sermon outlines for the whole Christian year.

He would poke gentle fun at these aids referring to 'Seed thoughts for busy sowers', 'Tips for tired toilers' and 'Treasures from the Tabernacle'. But the second article in his famous series 'Monday morning musings' was a little more serious. It concerned the true story of a young officer who slid into the practice of just before the meeting, tearing out the appropriate page in *The Officer* magazine containing sermon outlines and proceeding to present the most suitable one as God's word to his people.

'Like most "ready-mades",' observed 'Ensign' in October, 1930, 'it was ill-fitting in parts.' But with sympathy he continues: 'Let those who have never tried out a "ready-made" cast the first stone. I do not raise my hand. Those who have savingly accumulated over the years a stock of addresses must also forbear judgment. . . . But this lad is really on my mind . . . I foresee how rusted up his mind will be in fifteen years time. . . . Cannot someone tell him that to think, *to think*, TO THINK out his own ideas—slowly, awkwardly, painfully—is better than consulting whole shelves of printed outlines?

'The water of life which has stood so long in those vessels has grown cloudy. It has lost its first sparkling clearness. . . . But none of these metaphors which I have so badly mixed conveys the desperate urgency of forsaking those cisterns, which hold at the best but stale water, and resorting to the springs which bubble up from one's own deep broodings over Holy Writ.

'Study the masters of preaching by all means. But for inspiration, not for slavish imitation. . . . While a man may cheerfully own that he is a part of all whom he has met, the wise student will have so assimilated the mental food he has eaten that no acute listener will say "That is X, and that is Z". . . . No source of grist to the mill can be neglected. But to take in cold blood an odd outline, no matter from what source; and without previous study, to attempt to speak from it . . . ! may he never be pushed into that corner, for his very soul's sake, more than once in his lifetime . . . our best work is not borrowed, but is the fruit of our own labour, when in close company with the Holy Spirit we brood over some passage of Holy Scripture which we believe will be helpful to our people.'

'The only thing in Scripture that grew up overnight perished the next day,' he observed.

But he was not against help. 'My bucket has been stood under many taps—and will go on standing under many more. Turned full on, I ought to add.' One tap under which he, at an early stage in his officership put his bucket, was a book published by Hodder and Stoughton in 1923. It cost him four shillings—two weeks' pocket money in those days—in a second-hand book shop. Containing nearly 700 pages, this life of Alexander Whyte by G. F. Barbour influenced him greatly, dictating in some measure how he would prepare in the future. He never read without making notes, and tried never to let a day go by without preparing or studying something: 'In the mood or not in the mood, full of the joy of life or fed up to the back teeth, duty must be done. There is nothing to be done except to toil.'

One of the main reasons he thought there were so many poor sermons was that preachers put off their preparation until late on Friday night, and found themselves at panic stations looking at a blank piece of paper, 'despairingly casting around for some line of thought for Sunday morning' or contenting oneself with repeating old material. But he was not against repeating old sermons. A sermon entitled 'Put on the garments that suit God's chosen people' (Colossians 3:12, *NEB*) he first preached in Sydney in 1961, then in Collaroy in 1963, Singapore in 1967, New York in 1976 and at the International College for Officers in February 1980 for which occasion it was rewritten.

In his talks to officers, he told the story of that great preacher Campbell Morgan commencing his address on one occasion by saying: 'Open confession is good for the soul. So I might as well tell you before we start that I am preaching this sermon for the 119th time.' But Coutts advised that if a sermon was to be re-used then the officer should think of a better introduction, work on a more conclusive ending and add a new illustration. He knew that what was not fresh to the preacher could contain no freshness to the hearer therefore: 'I will have prayed the more earnestly that the Holy Spirit will breathe upon these dry bones and cause them to stand up, an exceeding great army.'

Another reason Coutts gave for poor addresses was that some preachers refuse to instruct themselves, or prepare thoroughly because 'the people don't want it', or 'can't understand it'. In answer to this argument he asked: 'If that had been Christ's attitude, would Jesus ever have opened his mouth?' But he also knew the tension of the officer who had studied and broadened his theological horizons being faced with a congregation which preferred what it knew, and no more.

Yet having studied was no reason to be ponderous: 'the true teacher is alert, lively, interesting, witty . . . knowledge will make him more interesting, not less. . . . True depth is so clear that one can see to the bottom through its transparent waters.' He was all too aware that what the preacher has not understood himself, he cannot possibly communicate to another. He was always angry with preachers who did that: 'Nothing goads me more than the speaker who says "I must leave you to think it out for yourself." What's he there for?' The last sentence is as important as the first. 'Why go out of one's way to dig up obscure texts from remote corners of Scripture (with little application to today) and ignore all that Jesus was and is and said and still can do? Without underestimating the powerful lessons to be gathered from the Old Testament I would like to hear more about Jesus, Saviour, Lord and Teacher, from our platforms.'

He lived by the principle that there was always something more to learn from the Scriptures, 'the source book of material for the Christian instruction of our people'. He had learned not to take anything for granted so far as Scripture was concerned. Neither was it a question of how much of the Bible could be read in the shortest possible time but how much of its content had become one's own, for the Bible has to be read devotionally as well as studiously:

> There should be some part of the day set apart where for fifteen/twenty minutes (or more, but hardly less) we set ourselves to go through a book of the Bible at a time, determined to pass no passage, no phrase, no word, until we know what it means and can express that meaning in our own words. As we are in this job for life, we have time for this method.
>
> Read aloud word by word, passing nothing until you know what it means and understand what it teaches. The opposite is the lucky dip method. This kind of slow but sure Bible study will steadily build up our biblical knowledge which, savoured by real life illustrations, drawn wherever possible from our own experience, helps to make our platform work scripturally accurate and livingly relevant.

As a child he had been set the standard of reading a chapter a day. Even in retirement he confessed that a chapter a day was too much. Even a few verses a day were too much. Sometimes he pondered a verse, or part of a verse, for several consecutive days until he had understood it and made it his own. 'I do not wolf down my food at the family dinner table. No more at the Lord's table. The test is: how much is now part of my spiritual blood stream? For this one does not need to know Greek or Hebrew; we can all read English. That is all I do. . . . It is my grasp of the Christian teaching of the word which provides me with material for the Christian instruction of my people.'

And in this regard he constantly proclaimed the use of modern translations. The translation was not important, but whether his hearers understood. 'Use them all,' he declared. One of his most cherished books was *The Twentieth Century New Testament*, inherited from his father, and inscribed and distributed by the Chief of the Staff in 1905. It had been published in 1904 and stood alongside eleven other translations of the Bible on his bookshelf.

Having studied and committed his thoughts to paper, there was the final preparation; just like his articles by 'Ensign', his sermons had to be 'boiled down'. These were then neatly typed on A4 paper cut in half horizontally. On the front would be his text. On the reverse side of this would be the list of places where the talk had been given:

New York	24.x.65
Berlin	xi.66
Peterborough (Ont.)	26.iii.72
Staple Hill	6.i.74 (rewritten)

This was a discipline he continued to the end of his life. On the second page the sermon would begin. The Coutts' disciple would hear his favourite phrases: 'So far so good'; 'Very well, then'; 'Be that as it may'; 'Fair enough'; 'I do not need to remind this congregation'; 'Again from our Sunday-school days we will recall'; 'Those of us who have read. . . .' They were all written down, even to: 'Pause here. And now our songster brigade will sing for us.' There was nothing left to chance—not even the words for which he 'searched' or hesitated over whilst speaking.

As a captain his sermon notes were complete: full sentences and references given for illustrations and quotations. Towards the end of his life, when his handwriting was legible only to himself, his preparation of the text from Matthew 19:27 received the same attention. First of all he took several sheets of A4 paper and filled them with notes. There were nine pages in all. These were edited and corrected. Modern translations were consulted and illustrations from Army history recorded. From those notes a first draft was typed with double spacing on A4 paper to make editing easier. Again he deleted and substituted words and phrases, changed a sentence and corrected spelling and punctuation. From this the final draft was typed again. This third and final version was again edited and polished. This by a man who had been speaking in public for sixty years and had addressed congregations of more than 10,000 people. His five-minute stories for the children, as retired General of The Salvation Army, were typed out word for word. The spiritual message for a child needs as much preparation as that for an adult, was his principle.

Coutts drew his illustrative material from his reading and from life: 'One cannot hope to grow either in mind or spirit without reading. If I am to serve God as I ought, I cannot at any time neglect the enrichment of my mind. This applies whatever our age. I was required to give attention to reading when I began in 1920. It was still a major commandment when I retired in 1969. And unless I continue to obey it I shall sink to the level of a record player. . . . One has to go on learning or it is death not life.'

Though an avid reader he did not consider it to be a superior activity for the corps officer over visiting: other work may not be neglected because of the need to read. 'I do not believe in rummaging around secondhand bookstalls,' he wrote. There was a need to read selectively, and in theology he read by author and not by attractive titles. Neither was one allowed to study in one's slippers, no one goes to work in their slippers, and study is work.

Especially to Army officers he commended Army books: 'Army illustrations from Army books, for Army addresses, delivered on Army platforms, by Army officers,' was his motto. 'Do not despise what comes out of Nazareth. Those who did set at naught their salvation.' Coutts saw the value of Army biographies in that they kept an officer's work in perspective, delivering him from the incredible notion that no one has ever had a heavier cross than his to bear; they gave a true understanding of prayer and the presence and protection of God.

He knew that the majority of salvationists did not know the history of their movement, so he could educate whilst safely using a story no one else had told. His greatest delight was when ultra-conservative thinkers said that things couldn't or shouldn't happen in the Army because it was against the spirit of the Founder. If he could prove from Army history that they were wrong, then he was quietly delighted. His Army illustrations were not only limited to the past. He would often refer to something he had read in that week's issue of *The War Cry* or *The Musician.* If he could make reference to the *Year Book* and *The Soldier's Armoury* he would.

His other illustrative material came from everywhere: Russian poets and authors with unpronounceable names; Peter Cook and Dudley Moore; military leaders and the Cruft's dog show; the world of classical music and current events; John Bunyan and Oscar Wilde.

In a sermon based on Romans 1:16 Coutts used a quotation from Vincent Van Gogh, the Dutch painter; the American writer Allen Drury; reference was made to the Australian author Patrick White, and to Ignazio Silone writing about Fascism in Italy. Though possessing a collectanea running into thousands of pages, assembled over fifty years, he rarely quoted more than one or two sentences from these literary treasures. This was because even illustrations must not get in the way of the message: they do not confirm a truth, they merely illuminate it.

If he considered preparation a hard and rigorous discipline he regarded the actual task of preaching as harder still: 'For by preaching I do not mean the dull drone of the man who is content to read an essay from the platform rail. Preaching is communicating the sense of the presence of the living God to a congregation and winning their assent to those eternal truths which have to do with their redemption. The motive of the preacher is the salvation of the hearer, and we can be content with nothing less than preaching which leads to an acceptance of Jesus as Saviour. We are pleading for a verdict in his favour. Any other kind of speaking may be learned and eloquent, but unless he stands—as John Bunyan said about the ideal minister—as one who *pleads* with men, then it is not preaching.

'This has little to do with our current conception of the delivery of an address to a congregation of converted people. Rather is it a declaration from the house tops of who God is and what he can do for the whosoever. It does not think of religion as an intellectual knot to be untied so that men may be convinced, but as a truth to be declared so that men may be convicted and be saved. . . . To preach is to communicate the life of God to those who are dead in trespasses and sin. . . . As only life can beget life, I cannot communicate it if it is not in me. . . . In every act of preaching I can give only such as I have,' Coutts declared.

He continued: 'Unless the wonder of God's love continually quickens my imagination and the sadness of man's sin stirs me to active compassion, unless I am careful, I shall end up by speaking of those things like a wearied child recites the multiplication table. . . . Continually I need to be made freshly aware, as if for the first time, of human need . . . at my desk, as I am wrestling to bring some truth to life, laying myself upon it as Elisha with the Shunammite's son, mouth on mouth, eyes on eyes, hands upon hands, half a dozen lines may cause a stir of life.'

A rare glimpse of this private petitioning was seen when thinking he was alone in a room prior to leading a meeting he was heard to say out loud in deep reverence: 'O Christ, help me.' At the moment of delivery he believed that he was not on his own. 'I may dare to apply to myself the word of our Lord in the Upper Room: "I am not alone, because the Father is with me". None of us is alone whether facing a congregation of twenty or 200. By his Spirit the Father is with us—not to enable us to demonstrate our command of the English language, nor to display our outstanding knowledge of the more obscure parts of Scripture . . . but simply to speak of the wonder of his grace.

'Once this true measure of my task dawns upon me I shall realise that my head and my heart are jointly involved. Of the two I may have more trouble with my heart. . . . My preparation of myself matters even more than the preparation of my material, though attention to either must never be made an excuse for neglecting the other. Yet though I may have built the altar with immense pains, laid the wood with every care, and made ready the sacrifice at great personal cost—the fire from heaven still needs to fall.'

Coutts' call to the mercy seat at the close of his meetings was considered by some not to be fervent enough. One Australian commented that he wasn't very good at drawing in the net. From time to time there are prayer meeting leaders in the Army, men and women who are particularly gifted at being able to lead a prayer meeting in such a fashion that many people move forward to the mercy seat to pray. Coutts did not possess that gift, nor did he employ any technique which placed people under any emotional pressure to respond to the Bible message. Prayer meetings were for prayer, and if no one came forward then the meeting would be closed, without any pressure being exerted.

His invitations to the mercy seat were not a repetition of his sermon: 'If there is anyone who would like to make an act of dedication or of obedience or of penitence—to give opportunity for this act to be made we shall sing. . . .' He prayed as sincerely after a meeting as he had done beforehand.

The result of exercised thought and meditation, Holy Spirit power and absolute literary discipline meant that Frederick Coutts brought light and inspiration to people of all ages throughout his ministry of preaching. He could distil great truth and present it for the simplest to understand. His messages encouraged and lifted peop[le] rather than continually pointing them to their weaknesse[s] and failures. His sorrow was that 'because so many sermons are dull—and I can say this because I bear my responsibility for a share, and for my sins I know many stories about dull sermons—we have come to the conclusion that Jesus was dull'.

Frederick Coutts had a reputation for being a gifted preacher, but this work was just one aspect of his concept of Army officership. He knew the limitations of preaching and that pastoral care was vital: 'What keeps men and women close to Christ is not spell binding, but caring . . . we are not remembered by what we said—that can be forgotten; indeed we have difficulty ourselves in remembering what we said—but by what we did. Preaching is not just an attempt to speak for twenty minutes to a captive congregation. Preaching is the round the clock example of the man or woman in whose heart the love of Christ has been shed abroad.'

Neither was the task of preaching to be considered more important than fund raising or attention to correspondence. It was part of the job. When invited to speak about the officer as teacher he listed all the activities of a corps officer whether his soldiery were few or many. The listed included everything from 'a judge or divider of men' to lighting the hall fire. If he was to talk about the officer as a teacher it was not that one of these aspects of officership was more important than the other, but it was a question of being 'selective' and he would be happy to return and speak about 'jumble sales, their cause and cure'.

In his appointment as territorial commander he knew of similar pressures: 'Salvation Army leadership is not only a matter of conducting a good meeting, leading a happy chorus, or even giving a thoughtful Bible address. These are all important parts of our calling, but I have ruefully reflected more than once that if all I had been required to do had been limited to the public platform, then life would have had far fewer worries.

'Some leaders love the field and hate the desk; others

nd love the desk. For some the problem-
sion-taking, letter-answering part of an
is a weariness to the flesh. If they receive
tates a problem which calls for a solution,
drawer in the hope that it will go away.
e a piece of fish, the longer it is left, the
more will it decay.

'I know from experience how difficult it can be to come
to a just decision. And even when one is doing what seems
in all honesty to be right, the consequences can be
personally unpleasant. But it is no use any officer asking
for larger responsibilities, and then complaining about the
increasing burdens.'

In accordance with the Army's constitution and the legal
provisions in the 1931 Act of Parliament, on Thursday 25
July 1963 the Chief of the Staff, Commissioner Erik
Wickberg, despatched to forty-nine Salvation Army
officers around the world the formal notice to be present
at 2 pm on Thursday 19 September at Sunbury Court, at
Sunbury on Thames, for the sixth High Council which
would elect the Army's eighth General. Commissioner and
Mrs Coutts and Elizabeth planned to sail to England via
the Pacific Ocean and through the Panama Canal.

Mrs Coutts was especially looking forward to the trip
because she would see her family again after six years.
Elizabeth who was now very Australian had gained a
modern languages degree and was teaching. Her plans
were to spend a year in Europe and then possibly return
to settle in Sydney.

Smallpox vaccinations were necessary for the journey,
an instruction duly observed by the family. That weekend
the commissioner was leading youth councils in Petersham
Town Hall in Sydney and the stiffness which Mrs Coutts
experienced in her leg was put down to the amount of
marching they had done that day. When she stood to pray
at the close of the day's meetings no one had any idea
that this would be 'her last public action in full possession
of her physical powers'.

When she awoke the following morning, Mrs Coutts was
paralyzed from the waist down. It was thought there

might be a growth on her spine trapping the nerve, but after many unpleasant tests in a large hospital nothing was found. On Tuesday 3 September Mrs Coutts was moved to the Army's Bethesda Hospital. It was out of the question that either she or Elizabeth would travel to London and on the following Monday Commissioner Coutts flew alone to London to help choose the next General.

CHAPTER NINE

Thy will be done

Once in London, Commissioner Coutts first visited his children: Margaret and Railton in St Albans and John and Heather who were on homeland furlough from Nigeria and staying at the Army's missionary flats in Highbury Grove, North London. After that he called in at IHQ. On the Saturday he was at Chalk Farm and on the Sunday he conducted meetings at the Regent Hall. The private welcome to the High Council took place on Tuesday 17 September at Caxton Hall, the public welcome in the Westminster Central Hall the following evening.

At 9.15 on Thursday morning 19 September, the day the Council was to begin, Frederick Coutts made a significant entry in his diary. It was six single syllable words, on two lines:

As Thou wilt,
Where Thou wilt.

Less than an hour before the Council was due to begin, General Kitching led a prayer meeting for officers and employees at IHQ, whilst at Sunbury Court, 'slightly anticipating the hour of two o'clock in the afternoon, sounds of devotional singing in a prayerful prelude filtered through the closed doors of the conference chamber', *The War Cry* reported.

The commissioners' discussions which preceded the actual election were concerned with the needs of The Salvation Army and considered under whose leadership these needs could best be met. Voting would not begin for another twelve days. The recurring theme was that of the things which the salvationist believes; the unshakable foundations of faith on which the Army was built and to which it still adheres. The hidden message was not so well camouflaged: everyone knew just what was being suggested. It was a thrust against a non-literalistic Bible interpretation and 'modernist' tendencies of which Coutts was considered by some to be a prophet.

Several officers not involved in the proceedings had circulated the members of the High Council with their views and concerns about modern trends in the Army's theology. One officer in particular prepared a fifty-page document attacking the unorthodox and unsound teaching which had come into the Army largely through the changing pattern of The *International Company Orders*— a book for which Coutts had been responsible as editor and as literary secretary.

Coutts had become the focal point of the tensions between conservative and more liberal theological schools of thought within the Army. However the youngest member of the Council, Colonel Tor Wahlström, the territorial commander for Denmark, prepared a series of more than adequate answers to these suggestions. There was no need for anyone else then to reply to that particular paper.

The decision as to who should be the next General was not easy. After several days of discussion one Council member confided: 'I must wait a little longer, pray some more, think more, listen some more before I make the mark on the paper which will be the best I can do in obeying the will of God.'

Gradually a picture emerged of the person needed to lead the Army through its centenary celebrations and into its second century. At noon, Monday 30 September, a statement was issued saying that the Commissioners W. Wycliffe Booth, Fredk L. Coutts, Edgar Grinsted, Glenn Ryan, Erik Wickberg and Lieut-Commissioner Clarence Wiseman had accepted nomination for election. The procedure was simple; following the answering of any questions submitted in writing by other Council members, one of the nominees must receive a clear two thirds majority. Each nominee was allowed a five minute speech without interruption of any kind, and with no expression

141

of approval or assent on the part of the listeners. There could be no cross examination of nominees arising from the written answers. Most of Coutts' twenty-seven written answers were shorter than the questions: three times a 'yes' and twice 'no'.

One aspect receiving close attention was, naturally, that of Mrs Coutts' health and her chances of recovery. Coutts, who had been pleased to accept nomination, did not try to hide what information he had. He believed that he had been given an honest medical opinion and that his wife would make a full recovery after suffering a post-vaccinal reaction.

The following day, Tuesday 1 October, as *The War Cry* reported, it was obvious to those waiting outside that there would be more than one ballot, especially when the afternoon session was broken for several minutes—with no one from inside the Council Chamber making contact with those outside. Voting commenced at ten minutes past two; after the fourth ballot, at 4.29 pm the final result was declared. The eighth General had been elected and only the legal formalities needed to be completed.

Commissioner Frederick L. Coutts had been elected but because that signature was not legal, he signed only Frederick Coutts on the deed of acceptance and only ever used that name afterwards. The chamber doors were opened to the press who had been waiting impatiently since two o'clock and the General-elect held the first of hundreds of press conferences he would have around the world as the Army's international leader: no, there were 'no immediate change of plans for the movement'; he wanted the Army to do what it was already doing, 'only to do it better'; he wanted a gospel that 'would apply to the intelligence as well as to the heart'. *The Times* of 2 October 1963, reporting the election said that 'the new leader was launched quietly and almost reluctantly'.

When the bombarding questions had ceased, the news-reel lighting turned off, and there was not a flashbulb to be seen or heard, the General-elect took tea with General Wilfred Kitching, and members of the High Council.

Perhaps there was never a more welcome cup of tea ever placed in the hands of Frederick Coutts. The General-elect reacted in his own special way: there was no evident emotion, nor enthusiasm. Neither was everyone happy about the decision either because of his theology or because of the implications to the office of the General should his wife remain physically disabled. Because of this, the Chief of the Staff came under some pressure, but nevertheless remained loyal to the General-elect and the decision of the Council.

On the night of Coutts' election, Captain Les Mingay had driven the General-elect to the radio and television studios after which Coutts asked to be driven to Highbury to see John and Heather again. The result of the election was hardly mentioned: there followed a silence and then another subject was sought. Returning to Sunbury in the early hours of the morning, the car stopped at some traffic lights by Trafalgar Square. A taxi drew up and the driver, recognising Coutts from the publicity, wound his window down and inquired: 'Aren't you the new General of The Salvation Army?' 'I'm afraid so,' replied Coutts deferentially. 'Don't worry, mate, you'll do alright!' and with that he drove away.

The Council over, Frederick Coutts, refusing an offer of help, cut a very lonely figure as he carried his own cases to the waiting car. But then his whole Generalship was to be a lonely pilgrimage—partly by force of circumstances and to a large degree by the nature of his character. He began and remained a very private General.

With Coutts, when something was finished it was finished: there was no harking back and he would busy himself with the next matter. Time was short: there were only eight weeks before the appointment came into effect on 23 November. He would return to Australia as quickly as possible, clear his desk in Sydney, pack, say farewell, and set out for London with his wife and Elizabeth, who least of all had expected that he would be elected. Upon arrival he found that the specialist had not even been to see Mrs Coutts as he had promised; it was only after he heard that Mrs Coutts was the wife of the General-elect that he came. Coutts did not care for this respect of persons.

If Elizabeth had not wanted to move to Australia as a teenager, she certainly wasn't happy about returning to England six years later. Her cosy life was shattered: there would again be big meetings and lots of travelling for the family. Mrs Colonel Harry Warren packed for the Couttses and a Salvation Army nurse, Captain Jean Watson, was released from Bethesda Hospital to accompany Mrs Coutts on the voyage and help settle her in the new quarters.

The atmosphere in Sydney was as if an Australian had been chosen and the General-elect received a tremendous territorial send-off in the packed Sydney Congress Hall. Speakers included the secretary of the Council of Churches in New South Wales whose president also prayed; the general secretary of the British and Foreign Bible Society and the general secretary of the Australian Council of Churches. The Deputy Lord Mayor of Sydney was there, but Mrs Coutts was unable to be present. There had been a move forward in every area of the work in that territory. In one territorial soul-winning campaign 3,500 mercy seat decisions were made, of whom 1,000 were by people new to the Army.

One retired officer began to write a farewell letter to Mrs Coutts from her Melbourne home, several hundred miles away from Sydney, when a bright idea occurred to her: 'I will put a stamp on myself and be both the message and the messenger.' She went to the airport, bought a ticket and within a couple of hours had presented herself at the Bethesda Hospital where Mrs Coutts was a patient. This was just one of the special tokens of appreciation shown to the farewelling territorial leaders.

It was a vastly larger crowd of salvationists which waved from the wharf at noon on Saturday 26 October 1963, than that which had greeted them on Sydney Central Station in 1957. Petersham Corps hired a ferry to follow the ocean liner, the band playing such melodies as the Founder's song and 'Waltzing Matilda' accompanied by the timbrels.

Mrs Coutts was not making the expected recovery and on board ship the only way she could move around was on an ordinary chair with castors because there were no facilities for a wheelchair. Throughout the voyage Coutts was working. Upon their arrival in England three weeks later, Coutts wrote to their ship's steward, Mr Latham, and after thanking him for his help added: 'Since arriving in England I have been receiving even more overseas stamps than ever, and I hope that the enclosed may reach you, for your daughter, before you sail again from Southampton.'

Between his election and his return to Britain the new International Headquarters at 101 Queen Victoria Street had been opened by Queen Elizabeth the Queen Mother, and during the first few weeks of his appointment the removal vans were still busy bringing the various departments of National and International Headquarters under one roof.

The first letter General Coutts wrote in office was addressed to General Wilfred Kitching (R).

My dear General,

    The first letter to be written after reaching International Headquarters must be one of thanks for all the arrangements made for the change-over both on the official and personal level. . . . You will find that I shall not be slow to acknowledge the way in which Mrs Kitching and yourself sought so energetically and earnestly to further what you saw to be the highest interests of the Army. . . . I am sure that a continued public welcome awaits you whenever you feel free to respond to such invitations.

And his appreciation was shown and a welcome was always extended just as he promised. He valued very much the trouble taken by his predecessor to set out his thoughts on the work and office of the General: 'I realise that no one can occupy this particular appointment for the shortest of terms without being the object of comment—some fair, and some unfair. But I have lived long enough to be able to treat this equably and set my

145

heart and mind on those things that are deemed to be the right and wisest for the work of God.'

The Couttses new home at Wallington was most unsuitable for anyone with a physical handicap, and there was central heating in only half of the house. John noticed that his father, now sixty-four years of age, was struggling to lift all the things officers have to unpack and store in their lofts ready for the next move. Coutts' own physical strength was diminishing at the start of his term of office whilst, in additional to everything else, his wife needed an increasing amount of attention.

At home Coutts wished to do everything himself—including the washing-up; letting someone else into one's home was an intrusion into one's privacy and besides, they would want to make conversation. He held off all offers of help. When the General was away for the weekend Margaret, with Ray, would go to look after her mother. Except for Mrs Crate, a salvationist at South Croydon who came in to clean, no other help was accepted, though a great deal was offered from many different people.

Even when matters became so difficult that in all reasonableness it was only right and logical that help should be provided he still insisted on nursing her, sometimes lifting her three times in the night to the bathroom. Despite an ulcerated leg he would still do his own shopping on a Saturday.

Right from the start, as far as the Army papers were concerned, there was a news embargo on Mrs Coutts' health. Even though the Army world would have shared, if only in prayer, the extra burden the General had to carry, salvationists were not allowed access into their private circumstances.

Apart from settling into his new appointment and discovering the administrative work of a General, there was the busy round of official welcomes to be made. Despite the genuine warmth of these welcomes, they were lonely occasions for him: Mrs Coutts could not be present for the official welcome to IHQ, nor at the Westminster Central Hall at which, in her absence, Elizabeth read a message from her mother:

I think you will understand my great regret at being unable to be present tonight. Quite apart from the pleasure it would have given me to see so many old friends again . . . it is not by my own desire that I am absent on this important occasion. There is one precious promise which I have been taking in a very literal sense in recent days—the familiar words found at the close of chapter 40 of the prophecy of Isaiah: 'They shall walk and not faint'. Knox translates this: 'They that wait upon the Lord shall go marching along'. This is what I hope to do in days to come, and if it is behind the Army flag and in front of an Army band, so much the better.

In his address 'Youth Aflame', Billy Graham quoted the principal of a famous American university as saying that everyone needs three things—a faith to believe, a flag to follow, and a song to sing. For me these three needs have been met in the service of God and the Army. . . . I have found that following Jesus—for me in the ranks of the Army—has given both aim and purpose and fulfilment to my life. . . . This is my desire in this new appointment—to proclaim God's love revealed in Christ with all my ransomed powers. I pray that God may lead everyone in this gathering into a like dedication to his will and purpose, and may his blessing rest upon us all.'

The General travelled alone to the other British Territory welcomes. Any sense of loneliness must have been heightened at Newcastle where the welcome meeting was held in the very hall in which he and Bessie married nearly forty years before. Busloads of salvationists hoping to attend the meeting had to be turned away because there was no room for them.

The Couttses became soldiers at South Croydon, a small London suburban corps where in his first official corps engagement as General he led the holiness meeting—again alone. But he was not just 'showing his face', he had stood earlier in the open-air meeting, as he had always done as soldier and officer alike, playing an E♭ bass. It was bitterly cold and the snow was falling. With the handful of bandsmen he marched back to the hall whilst Brigadier

Syd Woodall, his chauffeur, had gone on ahead in the car.

Coutts continued the same style of leadership he had adopted in Sydney: calling people by name and not just by rank—quite a departure from precedent; instead of sitting behind his large desk he would make a point of sitting beside his visitor in an easy chair; and he still wouldn't ask for the things he needed—thus causing many difficulties for the secretarial team which was there to serve him. He continued to leave his office and go in search of the person who could provide him with the information he needed. His secretariat would sometimes have to ring round IHQ asking: 'Have you got the General?'

In fact, such was the confusion that eventually he had to be politely asked to stay put and allow his team to bring him what he needed. Because he did not wish to promote himself, he therefore did not promote the office of the General. His self-introduction on the telephone was legendary: 'Coutts here.' Some felt that, in that respect, he did not do justice to the office; that he was behaving in an undignified manner and confusing people by such behaviour. Employees and officers did not know how to respond to a General who came to them rather than they being summoned.

One secretary complained that because the letters were addressed to him he felt that he had to answer them himself—typing his own replies as General. If dictation was a terrible experience for him, it was even worse for the secretaries. Apart from him seeming to dictate to the waste paper basket, one secretary receiving the letters had the feeling that because of the lengthy silences, her presence had been forgotten—but he was just choosing the right word. He was always looking for confirmation of facts and would often ask one of his secretaries to check the information for him. Later, he would ring the person himself, to confirm the confirmation.

The partnership of a General with his Chief of the Staff is crucial to the efficient running of the movement. When Coutts was elected, Commissioner Wickberg, who had already been Chief for two-and-a-half years, immediately offered to take another appointment. Coutts did not reply immediately but shortly after taking office went to the Chief and asked him if he still wanted a move. 'I want to offer you the choice of a Chief of your own choosing,' was the reply. 'Well, I'd be quite happy if you would stay on,' said Coutts quietly. And so an outstandingly strong and gifted administration was established. Their strength lay in their ability to allow each other the room to do their jobs properly, neither trying to do the other man's work.

Coutts' appeal was encapsulated in his intellect; as a writer and the public speaker who knew how to present not only the gospel in an intelligent fashion but could project the philosophy and purposes of The Salvation Army in a way no one else could. For this work he did not need other people: he was the master. Wickberg's gifts lay in his statesmanship and administrative prowess. The two men had completely different backgrounds and experiences, yet complimented each other perfectly.

Coutts, whose father had retired early because of illness after suffering the strains of early day corps officership, had himself spent several very successful years in corps work. As General he still had the heart of a corps officer. It was his essential nature.

Wickberg, the son of a Swedish commissioner highly regarded in Salvation Army circles, always regretted his lack of corps work experience, feeling that it was a missing element in his development as an officer. It was his three years as a divisional commander which he felt was the most formative and helpful preparation for his future appointments.

Erik Wickberg had worked at IHQ as a private secretary to an international secretary, and during World War Two had been responsible with Commissioner Karl Larsson for the European Salvation Army's liaison with London. Then he had been a chief secretary for nine years in two large territories and territorial commander in Germany. His appointment as Chief of the Staff, at fifty-seven years of age, following the sudden promotion to Glory of his predecessor Commissioner Norman Duggins, caused some surprise in the Army world.

He knew the structure of a territory and its relation to International Headquarters intimately. He knew the ins and outs of 'the building' as the headquarters was known, and he had for many years the experience of crisis management and the administrative problems which arise in Army life. Coutts had had none of this background. He was never an international secretary and had been a member of the advisory council to the General for only a few months before leaving for Australia as territorial commander.

There was also a sharp contrast in the basic mentality of the two men. For Coutts who had followed Gauntlett's thinking, all men were brothers and there were no barriers, no enemies and no foreign lands for the salvationist. This meant that any officer could be appointed to any country without creating any difficulties. There would always be a welcome for any officer by any group of soldiers because there was, so far as he was concerned, nothing which could divide Christians. Wickberg's experience had taught him otherwise. He was at home in the matter of making appointments and he knew that certain mixtures had to be avoided. Not all officers and territories were interchangeable. Wickberg was supported by a very special kind of secretary, Colonel John H. Swinfen, who though not a 'yes' man, and always speaking his mind, never leaked a syllable and would always follow the official decision even whilst disagreeing with it. He was a model of loyalty and a master of detail. The three men made a formidable trio.

Coutts and Wickberg did share a common love of books and study. Having left the training college each had discovered how inadequately those few months had prepared them for their future task. Whilst Coutts had been restricted to English literature and theological tradition, Wickberg had closely followed the European theologians and philosophers. Both were thirsty for knowledge, burning the midnight oil as young officers and keeping abreast of theological trends as leaders.

Despite the outstanding quality of their working relationship, never in those six years did they address each other by Christian names, and neither were the Wickbergs entertained in the Couttses home. Coutts' private and public lives remained, in that regard, totally divorced. Just as he did not talk about the Army at home, neither did he speak of his domestic difficulties in the office. Of that extra burden which was his own, he shared with no man.

Coutts was neither comfortable nor confident with administration. He didn't like making changes or giving promotions. He never moved until he was completely sure: he dared not take risks. He also failed to see that by using the authority of his office he was not pushing himself; that he could do things and make decisions as the General without bringing himself into the spotlight. It was as if something in him could not cope with that aspect of his appointment.

Apart from certain matters in which a principle was concerned—and Coutts could be very firm in such matters—the General left any disciplining to his Chief: Coutts was not at ease with that responsibility either. Neither was he at home in the world of the cut and thrust of appointments which some leaders relish. Painfully, Wickberg would try to prise a decision from him. The international secretaries needed patience when waiting for him to speak his decision: the process was slow and cautious. Proposals would be made, supported by the necessary information. The General pondered, and pondered.

But this is not at all surprising. The majority of his working life had been within the very specific discipline of words; he was never quite sure of himself as an administrator. It is a rare spirit indeed who can combine the reflective quality of a scholar, the creativity of a writer and the dynamic decisiveness of a top administrator. Perhaps it was for this reason that he regarded the workings of the Advisory Council to the General so highly. He felt safe in deferring decisions to that group of commissioners, knowing that several minds were better than one, and that their experience was greater than his. He never took a decision without consulting his Chief of Staff.

A chance remark about modern evangelism in a press conference held within hours of his election brought into being a Salvation Army phenomenon which became known as the Joy Strings. The heart of what Coutts said was that if alongside the traditional brass band it was necessary to take up the electric guitar and go into the coffee bars to reach the people with the gospel, then salvationists would do that.

The press seized upon it and wanted to see the principle in action—but what was there to see? There was a grass roots movement for a new kind of music within the Army and Major Fred Brown, the youth club secretary at Thornton Heath, had brought a number of musicians together for meetings aimed at teenagers. Though the performances were somewhat crude, the meetings were packed.

As a result of the media's attention, General Coutts called the training college for help. Captain Joy Webb and others who could play a few chords on a guitar were assembled for the BBC's *Tonight* television programme on which they sang some choruses and a few songs. They hadn't got a drummer—so Wycliffe Noble a young salvationist architect was asked to join the ad-hoc group.

Following the television appearance, several companies showed an interest in recording the group and within a short time the Joy Strings were cutting a demonstration disc at the EMI studios in Abbey Road. EMI decided to release the record immediately and 'It's an open secret' went into the charts. The group went on to accomplish a significant work especially amongst the unchurched.

Though the Joy Strings evolved in General Coutts' term of office they were not his idea, nor did he supervise their further operations. Who actually created the Joy Strings remains a discussion point: was it the media, the television programme, the record company—or divine initiative? However Coutts came in for a great deal of criticism for this suggestion which through force of circumstances had become reality.

Letters arrived on the General's desk from around the world. Some commissioners wrote privately expressing their unhappiness about the Joy Strings. Other leaders wanted to immediately establish orders and regulations for these groups and one commissioner would have much preferred the group to be called the Salvation Guitarists.

Some traditional brass band fanatics could not or would not be pacified with the idea that the two music forms could live in harmony; there was uproar in the Army musical world which polarised over the whole affair. There were some young people who could not believe that the General could sanction such 'immoral', 'devilish', 'passion-arousing' music. There seemed to be an internal civil war. Frederick Coutts took the time to answer each letter of complaint with courtesy, sympathy, and understanding, whilst remaining unmoved in his total support for the group.

The other backroom boys with whom he had worked in the literary and editorial department, discussed and developed ideas about life and God and the Army, were now expecting that their kingdom had come. They were looking to Coutts for the kind of leadership which had been inherent in all that they had spoken about in the tea-club.

Others who had been staunch disciples of 'Ensign' were looking for that same spirit in Coutts' new appointment. They were to be sadly disappointed. That anticipated freedom and opportunity never materialised and they felt let down. Coutts knew that there is a degree of liberty related to any and every appointment as a Salvation Army officer; and that a person is fully justified in exercising that degree of liberty to its limits. But then, he said, one discovers that the higher up you go in the Army, the more confined is your area of liberty. You are compelled to contract and work within the limited scope of that appointment and the office of the General is the most limited of all.

The editorial and literary department had seldom had a sterner taskmaster. He kept an unusually keen eye on what was written and presented for publication and went through the proofs as if still a member of the department. It became such a problem that the editor-in-chief and literary secretary, Commissioner A. J. Gilliard, had to go to the General's office to remind him that he was now the General and no longer the literary secretary. During the six years that Coutts was General there were no significant moves or promotions for the members of that department.

Some say it was because he knew them, and what they thought, so well that he dared not 'bring them on'. Others suggested that because he did not wish to be seen to be bestowing favours on his friends he treated them harder than those with whom he had had no real contact.

Articles, ideas or theological opinions likely to disturb or cause difficulties in other lands were altered or taken out. As General he had perceived the problems which could be caused when certain points of view were expressed. He was now the Army world's spiritual leader and did not want one simple comrade to stumble by reading what was published in his name. He could not bear that responsibility.

In the matter of Salvation Army history, however, he promoted a new sense of reality unknown before in the movement. The biography of George Scott Railton entitled *Soldier Saint* by Lieut-Colonel Bernard Watson had only one condition placed upon it by General Coutts: if Watson could prove it, then it would be published.

More importantly Coutts' personal drive, energy and dedication to the production of a new *Handbook of Doctrine* brought about one of the most significant publications within the movement. His utmost care and consideration in the realisation of this project should not be underestimated. It was he who when he had any spare moments revised the *Handbook of Doctrine* as he travelled the world. Even though a doctrine council had been engaged in its revision, when he took office he started again from scratch. He went to a lot of trouble to receive the opinions of all the international leaders who reported back in detail. It seemed that he discussed each line with the chairman of the council, Commissioner Herbert Westcott.

Though Coutts was a rebel accepted into the fold he

154

never fully revealed what his deepest opinions were about theology and politics in the six years he was General.

If an officer has failed to study before he comes to an important public office, it is then too late to begin. He cannot win back the time he lost. Within a short time people have the measure of any officer who often has to speak in public. They know whether he has prepared or not, is well read or not. In that sense there is nothing which remains hidden. One of the quotations in Coutts' massive collectanea illustrates the principle. In one of his penetrating studies of military character Liddell Hart has these sentences: 'When officers reach the higher posts, they have, in most instances, greater freedom from detail. But in actuality their time is so occupied . . . that the opportunity to study . . . is more than ever restricted even when the inclination survives. This, of course, is the fate of anyone who rises to prominence in any career, and it is rare for such a man to have the resolution to ration his engagements for the purpose of continuing his studies. . . . The short hours spent in study decrease as responsibilities increase.'

This was a strange quotation for Coutts to keep for if anyone seemed not to have the facility to refuse speaking engagements it was he. He would be conducting meetings as often as he possibly could. Brigadier Woodall, his driver, had never worshipped in so many churches and cathedrals as he did when serving General Coutts. Invitations were accepted from schools and colleges; there were visits to the several headquarters in London as well as corps, divisional and national events in the British Isles and the international tours planned as part of his Generalship.

The principles which decided whether or not he would accept an invitation were formulated early in his officership: if the invitation came; if the date was free and if he had time to prepare, then for the sake of the Army he would say yes.

He was preparing his initial material often months ahead. In his bag there would be four or five large brown envelopes on which were stencilled in large letters the name of an event, the city or land to be visited.

Brigadier Woodall and the General travelled in the car in silence—and if he had taken anyone along as a guest the silence still prevailed. It was possible to travel 200 miles to an appointment and 200 miles back without an exchange of conversation except across the tea-table at the billet and his usual, 'Goodnight, Syd. Usual time in the morning.'

During the journey Coutts would be reading, preparing, or carefully tearing out a newspaper article to put in the envelope. Ideas, quotations, notes, anything he could use at that particular occasion would be safely stored away. When the event had taken place he neatly crossed the name through and added another under it. One envelope began FILEY, then CLACTON, FINLAND and lastly BRENGLE.

With Coutts there was never any last minute desperate, wild searching for texts, the right illustration or other supporting material: he had already been focusing his attention on what he should say for many weeks. He was conscious of the enormous responsibility which was his when preaching. The last thing he would do before going into a meeting would be to sit in the front seat of the car and again go through his notes with his black pen, eliminating a phrase here, changing a word there, generally tightening up even further an already 'tight' construction.

That the truths he proclaimed touched his own heart could be heard in his delivery, but the tension of those larger occasions cost him more dearly than most people could imagine. Once, in Manchester, he left the meeting, very agitated and was very sick. However within ten minutes he was back on the platform and preaching. On another occasion, when journeying back from Scotland he began shaking quite badly—offering his excuses to his companion he said it would pass and he would be alright in a moment. It was a nervous reaction to the meetings he had just led. Arriving home after big meetings he would single-mindedly make a cup of tea and get to bed as quickly as possible—these were the two things which restored him.

CHAPTER TEN

In journeyings often

A General of The Salvation Army has more than a full-time job just coping with all the administration that goes with the appointment: an endless flow of correspondence and reports; matters of finance and personnel affecting the Army world; policy-making decisions; the thrashing out of problems which may have political, legal or ethical consequences; maintaining bridges to other Christian traditions; after dinner speaking, and the steady flow of invitations to attend all kinds of functions in a representative capacity. The Salvation Army is managed through regular discussions with the Chief of the Staff, the international secretaries and territorial leaders. There are consultations with numerous advisory bodies and, when necessary, officers with a specialist training. Missionary officers leaving or returning to their appointments are interviewed by the General. All that is published in the General's name crosses his or her desk. There is a steady flow of requests for letters, articles and introductions to special Salvation Army anniversaries or occasions. A General's pen is never still and there is little respite from the demands of the office.

Apart from all that a General is expected to travel: to rally the troops, inspiring them in the salvation war. The only way that a General can fully understand a particular situation is to see it for his or herself. Such tours are planned years ahead and Coutts did not let his soldiers down. In his six years as General he visited approximately forty countries, mostly without his wife. It was only towards the end of her life, when very poorly and in hospital, that Mrs Coutts declared: 'Frederick, if you would just stop jaunting around the world, I could be at

157

home.' When he was away the General provided her with a map and timetable so she was able to show her visitors just where he was and what he was doing.

General Coutts travelled with his private secretary, firstly Lieut-Colonel Gordon Barrett, then Major, later Brigadier, Edward Hodgson. With them travelled the respective international secretary and territorial leader or officer commanding. On these occasions the General did not regard himself as a tourist—rarely, if ever, taking a camera with him. When invited to see one of the country's most beautiful, inspiring or impressive sights, he usually refused for himself, but suggested the others might like to go. He wished to save his strength for the meetings and would retire to his hotel room or some quiet corner with a copy of *The Times*, his books, and make only one request, that tea might be provided. Frugal habits remained. On his travels he slit open used envelopes and recorded quotations on the inside for future use. And there must always be time for him to meet his officers.

The shorter hops to Europe presented no particular problems. Paris, Brussels, Amsterdam, Stockholm were just an hour or two's flying time from London. But tours to Africa or India did present difficulties for him at home. In this respect he made shorter tours than was usual (though one was a round trip of 38,000 miles) so he could be back at home as quickly as possible. In between Canada, Zambia, Japan, Peru, Singapore, Pakistan, Australia, the United States of America, there were visits to the small corps of Limehouse in the east end of London, Westminster Abbey, Southwark Cathedral, the International College for Officers, field officers councils at Swanwick, Campfield Press, Tollington Park School, Eltham College, and Balham Congregational Church.

One Sunday he invited himself to six London goodwill centres where he taught in the Sunday-school and played the piano for the children so they could sing some choruses. He visited sea-side corps to acknowledge the faithful witness and extra-mile service the soldiers gave during the summer. In youth councils he was masterly; and when attending the national over-60 rally at Clapton

Congress Hall he confessed he was happy to be amongst his own age group.

He returned to his old school, Leith Academy, to address a thousand pupils and there was a thrilling homecoming when in July 1964 the Couttses were able to visit Warrington together—Mrs Coutts' first weekend campaign outside London for more than a year. The mayor was also a bandsman and Frederick Coutts was always so proud when salvationists did well in the world of education or politics. The doxology was sung three times at the end of the Sunday meetings. A Rolls Royce, offered by a local businessman for use by the General and his wife that weekend, was graciously declined.

On one African tour, the government put a plane at the General's disposal which in one hour's flying time saved him a full day's travel of 300 difficult miles. However, amongst those who came to listen to him were those who had walked two days to be present. Practically the whole congregation of 500 knelt around a table which became a mercy seat. On another occasion Coutts travelled 1,400 miles by car and plane to lead just one meeting. At another centre salvationists camped for four days, holding a series of 'warming up' meetings in preparation for his visit. On these tours roll call would be at 5.30 am and it might be 9 pm before the party arrived back at the billet having travelled hundreds of miles by plane; addressed all kinds of meetings; met all kinds of people and inspected all kinds of buildings.

In non-European lands he was extra careful not to create the impression that the Army in any way supported the system of apartheid. Taking his concern sometimes to the extreme and causing unnecessary tension, he was never comfortable in a 'Europeans only' setting—and that applied not only to the African continent. When visiting Rhodesia he was asked to lead a Sunday night meeting at a 'European corps'. He was not happy. 'Am I to understand that there will be Africans present?' 'Yes, General, a good representation. They have been invited.' 'I want one to take part.' And so it was arranged that an African would read from the Scriptures. That night he took for his sermon Peter's vision recorded in Acts 10:15: 'What God hath cleansed, that call not thou common.' He made his point in every way, except to use the term 'apartheid' directly. He emphasised that the Army is for everyone, everywhere at all times, irrespective of class or colour, but in this instance he generated a lot of tension by doing so.

Travelling to Aba in Eastern Nigeria, the General took with him Brigadier Ephraim Zulu, a divisional commander from South Africa, who was descended from royal Zulu blood: 'I have brought him with me as a public witness of the place we want to give the African officer in the corporate life of The Salvation Army,' he explained. He believed that Africa was a continent belonging to the African and in which the Army was at work by the will and consent of the people.

In the same territory, the General's son, Captain John Coutts, BA (Oxon), BD (Lon), was the principal of The Salvation Army's secondary school at Akai. John's wife, Heather, was due to give birth to their second child a few weeks after the General's visit, but by some 'wonder' their daughter was born a little earlier than expected and General Coutts had the pleasure of dedicating his granddaughter, Marion, to God in a lovely palm grove, in the presence of the pupils and students.

Some extensive tours lasted several weeks during which he never repeated a sermon or lecture, and in which the congregation could be small or more than 10,000 people. Added to that were the annual, traditional British events attended by the General and/or the Chief: the day of meetings at Westminster Central Hall held each autumn, the carol services, and the commissioning being just a few. If there was no respite from the office, there was no release from the pressures of public speaking either.

Whether under an equatorial sun, amongst poverty and disease in a refugee camp or in the sophisticated and richer countries of the western world, the tours had much in common. They consisted of long days full of meetings, press conferences with the same old questions, the opening of new buildings or the laying of foundation stones, and the joy of swearing in new soldiers. On an American tour, in the midst of swearing-in 200 soldiers he read from the *Ceremonies Book*: 'In the name of the General—oh, my word!' he exclaimed. The congregation saw the humour immediately and after the laughter died away he added: 'Well, as they say "it's in the book" and the book can't be wrong.' He was as amused as his congregation—whether in private or public his humour was never far away. Often he was never more serious than when he was joking.

Though it was hard work, he did not mind the tours of institutions and hospitals because he knew that for the officer in charge it might be the only time in his or her life that they would see a General. At the other end of the scale there were receptions and lunches; audiences with civic and church leaders, politicians, heads of state and royalty.

Coutts thoroughly researched The Salvation Army's history in the areas he visited, be they small corps or vast countries, such as Canada, and always managed to identify himself with, or show appreciation for, a pioneer salvationist, a trophy of grace, or some sacrificial service. If possible he would mention an important incident from the Army's life and witness there. This stratagem never failed to get the people on his side.

The personal cost of those years for a man who refused all help in his private life, was approaching seventy years of age, and nursing a physically handicapped wife at home will never be known. He carried it all by himself. He was very private in all matters.

Wherever he went he never forgot his friends or comrades from the past. He would leave the platform after a meeting and speak to those who had been faithful soldiers in his corps appointments. He never forgot them, nor their names and never failed to greet them. He knew that it was the faithfulness of such soldiers that kept the Army alive. The General was conducting congress meetings in Scotland when one of the older comrades from Clydebank, with whom he had been friendly as a young man, was close to dying. Several days later a letter arrived:

161

Dear Edgar,

I was very sorry to learn that you are so unwell, and I want you to know that Mrs Wallis and yourself are very much in our thoughts and prayers at this time. I wish I had been able to come and visit you—but time did not allow me to do this. All the same, I met many of the Clydebankers. . . .

From the moment Coutts was elected General, Mrs Coutts was determined to play as full a part in their joint responsibilities as possible. It was decided that she would attend IHQ three days a week and be assisted by Lieut-Colonel Margery Joy. But Mrs Coutts generated so much work that the colonel had a full-time job assisting her. Mrs General Coutts wanted to be part of everything and was not content to allow others to take over any aspect of her work. She never said that she was too ill, or too tired to carry her work-load. However she was not an office person. Her desk was never tidy for long, and as she looked for correspondence or information, the carefully filed material gradually became so jumbled as to become a secretary's nightmare.

The colonel's patience with and service to Mrs Coutts was always recognised by the family who often joked about the time she was on her knees in the office with papers spread all over the floor trying to sort things out for their mother. They also knew that the colonel was a pretty good hand at signing 'B. L. Coutts'. One day the General let it be known to his team that the following morning Mrs Coutts would be walking into the office instead of using her wheelchair. No one argued of course for both the General and his wife were fiercely independent and strong personalities. It seemed they wanted to make a statement by this action. The General's car drew up just as officers and employees were arriving for work. With slow, painstaking movements, it took Mrs Coutts a full ten minutes to walk the few metres from the car to the lift. The exercise was never repeated.

Whenever possible, Mrs Coutts travelled with her husband. This meant traditional venues were sometimes changed to allow her wheelchair access onto the platform. These journeys included visits to America and Finland. Each year she visited the homes for retired officers in Britain and lectured regularly at the International College for Officers, as is the tradition. She also carried out her own special ministry of letter writing.

Correspondence which began as a business-like acknowledgment became newsy, lively letters. People knew she read her post by the replies they received. She visited a south London school to speak to a Christian fellowship in which a young teenage salvationist was active; there were home league occasions—she did all that was humanly possible to be by her husband's side. There was an offer of treatment from America; she visited the famous spa centre of Bath, in the west of England, for hydrotherapy. Courageously, Mrs Coutts travelled three times to a medical centre for remedial therapy in Switzerland to take a course of intensive treatment which seemed to do her good: 'What our future life will be will depend upon the results of this, as we are not without hope that our faith may be rewarded', Coutts affirmed. 'Certainly neither my wife nor myself have any interest whatever in any form of semi-invalidism.'

To confirm this determination, walking bars were placed in their quarters and exercise bars in her office at IHQ. Because of the open character of the platform at the Royal Albert Hall and other centres, the General invested time and energy in trying to find a more suitable wheelchair and something to replace the unsightly and heavy caliper splints she had to wear.

Whilst in Nigeria, John and Heather were never told by his parents about the full extent of Mrs Coutts's illness. The word paralyzed was never used. It was only via a third person that John discovered just how severely handicapped his mother had become. But that was in keeping with the General's thinking: he didn't pass his personal problems on to others.

*　　　*　　　*

In the world of association of ideas, when the

salvationist says Frederick Coutts, he immediately thinks 'centenary'. It seems that General Coutts was born to lead the 100-year celebrations of The Salvation Army, which reached their peak in London between Thursday 24 June and Saturday 3 July 1965. All his literary skill, his gift of communication, his knowledge of Scripture and the Church, his love of Salvation Army history and the Founders of the movement fused in those ten days to make such a deep impact upon the international Army and its friends.

Upon taking office in 1963 he straightaway became involved with the planning of centenary events. There was not a great deal of time and there was much to be done. Though delegating, his independent nature led him to show too much interest in the smaller details which he should have left to others. His 'interference' was from the highest of motives. He was going to make sure that nothing could possibly go wrong.

The following year, 1964, he used the Army press to full advantage to generate enthusiasm and supply information. The media showed growing interest and the number of magazines and newspapers which asked for articles and interviews increased dramatically. Though always courteous and friendly towards the reporters there were times in his Generalship when he could not hide his irritation with the press. When one journalist asked whether Christ had anything to do with the Army's record of successful service Coutts replied with an unusually forceful response. 'We work in the name of Christ, for the sake of Christ, at the command of Christ, and by the power of Christ.'

When asked about the Army's relationship to the churches he replied that it was his intention 'to confirm the faith of the Army in its place and function in the Church universal'. He believed that the churches and the Army would gain by closer co-operation. This however was not a view shared by everyone, amongst whom was the former Archbishop of Canterbury, Lord Fisher. In his autobiography *No Continuing City*, Coutts records something of their correspondence over the matter. It seemed that Fisher did not accept the Army as a church.

Neither was the desire for the Army to take its place within the Church always happily received by others—for different reasons. The Rev Dr D. Martyn Lloyd-Jones, the famous preacher of Westminster Chapel, who drew crowds to a congregational church near to Victoria Station, in London, wrote the General in 1967: 'I am however somewhat troubled by what I have been reading recently about the association of The Salvation Army not only with the Ecumenical Movement but also with the Roman catholics. . . .'

Coutts was impatient with the general assumption amongst journalists that The Salvation Army was a Victorian relic which could not possibly survive in a modern world. To this he would reply that 'so long as human need exists, there—as it shall please God—will be the Army'. He did not like the uninformed questioner who presupposed that every bandsman was a reformed drunkard or that the majority of soldiers were uneducated. Yet he would patiently explain time and time again the Army's reasons for its uniform, its flag and its mode of worship.

Should a reporter ask an awkward question he would first of all remove the sting; point out the emotive word and deal with it; and finally examine the hidden assumption before answering. He possessed a marvellous gift of saying nothing very well if the occasion demanded, even addressing another topic completely as a tactic to avoid falling into a trap. It was only afterwards that the less astute reporter realised he had received no answer at all.

A typical reaction of the more thoughtful was that of L. J. A. Bell writing for a Scottish magazine. 'When it was first arranged that I should meet the new General of The Salvation Army, somehow I did not expect to encounter anyone so humble. . . . I was left with the sense that I had met a man of sincere modesty, whose decided gifts never led him at any time to expect promotion to the rank of General, supreme leader of a world-wide organisation, or indeed to be a leader of anything.'

Because four-fifths of the Army's international strength was outside Great Britain, General Coutts was determined that the celebrations would be international in character: 'To limit our International Centenary to the United Kingdom would be to do the most serious injustice to the man to whom one European said: "Mon Général, you belong to the world."' Schemes were launched to finance salvationists from poorer countries so that William Booth's Army could properly be represented. The General asked salvationists to brush up on their knowledge of William and Catherine Booth so that 'Our own hearts might catch afresh something of the devotion of these two people to their Lord, to their work and to each other.'

Coutts was concerned that the festivities should also have some lasting effect, and that 1965 would represent something more than just a salvationist jamboree. The idea came from the Chief of the Staff that perhaps something could be done for the number of social institutions needing renovation or new accommodation.

At the same time Lieut-Colonel Arnold Brown was transferred from Canada to the public relations department at International Headquarters and was given the responsibility of establishing advisory boards as they functioned in Canada and America. The result of all this was the eventual 'For *God's* sake, care!' campaign, including the production of the book *Tragedies of Affluence,* which appealed for £3,000,000 from the British public for capital funds for social schemes, the first appeal having been made by William Booth in 1890. 'There is only one thing for a salvationist to write about, to talk about and to pray about in 1965,' wrote Coutts in the *Assurance* magazine, 'and that is the centenary.'

The summer centenary celebrations of 1965 were the high point of Coutts' Generalship: he had the right word for each occasion. The salvationist was justifiably proud of his leader. The General's intense longing for the Army to be recognised by the world-wide Church and for the soldier to recognise his own place in that Church came to fruition in the Royal Albert Hall on Thursday 24 June. In that inaugural meeting Her Majesty Queen Elizabeth

II took her place on the platform with the Archbishop of Canterbury (Dr Michael Ramsey), the Archbishop of Westminster (Cardinal John Heenan), the Moderator of the Free Church Federal Council (the Rev Peter McCall). Also present was the Home Secretary (Sir Frank Soskice, QC) and ambassadors and consular representatives of every country in which the Army was working. Church and state had come together to show their acceptance of the Army.

The teenager who had been incapable of giving his testimony in a corps meeting was now addressing his monarch, the country's religious leaders, political representatives and thousands of salvationists in an overflowing Royal Albert Hall. Here was a living testimony to what God's grace could do in and through a man, despite his essential nature. Coutts was brilliant and inspired. The ensuing week was full of all kinds of festival, meetings, rallies and pageants. Not least of these events was the great field day held at Crystal Palace attended by an estimated 50,000 people. It was a marvellous success; what few knew was that Coutts had not wanted to stage such an event, and was not at all convinced about it.

On Friday afternoon, 2 July, Founder's day, a Meeting of Thanksgiving was held in Westminster Abbey. The Army flag was processed to the high altar by men and women salvationists from many countries and Commissioner W. Wycliffe Booth unveiled a memorial to the Founder. The General's words in the Abbey have entered Army history, and engraved themselves on the hearts of those present. It was his introduction which made such an impact. But by what right was William Booth being honoured in the coronation church of sovereigns? 'By what right William Booth? To which the answer is: by no right—but by the grace of God. God's grace was not given to him in vain. With the Apostle he would have said: "By the grace of God I am what I am." . . . by that same grace we may become what God would have us be.'

The Salvation Army had been born in the open air and it was a fitting close to the celebrations in London that on Saturday 3 July thousands of salvationists marched along Whitehall, to an open-air meeting in Trafalgar Square in which officers from the Netherlands, Japan, Canada and a local officer from Africa took part. Frederick Coutts felt completely at home for he was preaching the good news in the open air, surrounded by people from many nations none of whom felt that they were foreign.

Coutts expressed his own purpose for the thirty principal meetings as 'designed to be a demonstration of the continuing spiritual life of that part of the universal Church of God known as The Salvation Army, with particular reference to our principles and practices. Under God this would be a confirmation to salvationists everywhere of their own faith, as well as a public witness to the truth that we who in time past were not a people were now a people of God to show forth the praise of him who had called us out of darkness into his marvellous light.'

In October of that year in another open-air meeting, this time held in San Francisco, all these elements were combined: 'This religious meeting commenced with the local monsignor offering the invocation and concluded with the benediction pronounced by the President of the Californian State Baptist Association. I said my piece in the middle and was not conscious of bowing either to the left or to the right. . . . But let there be no doubt—Jesus Christ was preached.'

During the first years of its life the Army expanded at such a rapid rate that the General inevitably became involved in centenary celebrations overseas, as well as in other departments of Army life in Britain. He was also personally honoured. In May 1965 he was granted the Freedom of the Burgh in Kirkcaldy, the place of his birth. On 10 May 1966 in the chapel of the Chung-Ang University, General Coutts was honoured with a doctor of letters degree.

The idea behind the popular and long running radio programme *Desert Island Discs* is that a celebrity is cast away on a desert island with only a gramophone, eight records, a Bible, the complete works of Shakespeare, a book of their own choice, and one luxury item to see him or her through the ordeal. General Coutts was invited to be cast away.

The programme presenter was Roy Plomley who, in his book *Desert Island Discs*, records the occasion:

I have great respect for The Salvation Army, who invariably offer help before they ask questions, and we invited General Frederick Coutts to take part in celebration of the Army's centenary in 1965. I gave him my usual telephone briefing, emphasising that we wanted a completely personal choice of music, and that he had the entire resources of the BBC Gramophone Library to draw on. I was a little shaken to see that the list of discs he afterwards sent me consisted of eight items by Salvation Army bands, choirs and groups. Could a man really be so single-minded in his personal musical choice?

At our recording session, he changed his mind about two of the Salvation Army discs, substituting the Glasgow Orpheus Choir singing 'By Cool Siloam's Shady Rill' and Sir Malcolm Sargent conducting the Berlioz overture, 'Le Carnival Romain'.

The opening question was asked, 'Are you a gregarious man and would solitude worry you more, do you think, than most men?' If the question was interesting to those who knew that he could travel hours without speaking to his companions and with whom it was sometimes purgatory to share a meal, the answer was quite a revelation: '. . . I do know I like to be with people and to mix with people and I might find it a bit hard to be on my own. I am not very good company just by myself.'

His final choice of record was the last verse of the Founder's Song, 'O boundless salvation', as arranged by Dean Goffin for the centenary service of thanksgiving held in Westminster Abbey. His book was *The Oxford Dictionary of Quotations* and his one luxury was a metal Salvation Army crest made and presented to him by a man at Miracle Valley, a social services centre just thirty miles outside Vancouver.

In the Queen's Birthday Honours list of 1967, General Coutts was appointed as a Commander of the Order of the British Empire. When his family rang to ask what it was all about, having learned the news from their morning paper, 'What medal?' was his reply. He hadn't even told his wife of the impending honour. Many letters of congratulations arrived on his desk and each received a reply in which he deflected the glory away from himself to the Army and the social services in particular:

'I appreciate your kind remarks regarding the Honours List, but this was really an acknowledgment of the current developments of our community services here in Britain.'

'I am not so lost to a sense of proportion as to suppose that this came to me on my account! But I value your good words none the less.'

'Between you and me, this CBE has little to do with me personally but is rather a recognition of the current advances we are trying to make in this country in the field of social services.'

'An old salvationist like yourself will know that this was not for me personally. It is a recognition of the continuing effort by the Army to meet human need in the community of our own day, and it is only in this sense that I could accept the appearance of my name in the Honours List.'

In July of that year Mrs General Coutts, at her husband's side, fulfilled her last public engagement, in Finland, at the territorial congress. A malignancy had disclosed itself and on his return from South America early in September, he knew Bessie was dying. 'It was a case of doing one's best to keep up appearances for my wife's sake, who was continually sustained by the thought of recovery,' he wrote. 'However this was not to be.' Secondary growths were seen on later X-rays and he was advised that it was 'unwise' to seek out the primary.

Professional help now had to be organised. Elizabeth who was still at home could do no more than she was already doing, so in November it was agreed that a Swiss nurse, Captain Marianne Berner, a friend of the family for many years, should come and look after Mrs Coutts from 10 December to 8 January. 'Dear Marianne,' wrote the General, 'Mrs Coutts has been in hospital for some weeks now. She is weaker than she was when she last came to Switzerland and, before I left for South America in August, it needed both Margaret and myself to help her. However, Margaret has her own home and children and this could only be a temporary arrangement.

'It is thought that a change from hospital might be a welcome one so far as my wife is concerned, and the doctors have agreed to this provided we can secure adequate nursing help. This is why I am so glad that you can be with us over these weeks at Christmas time.

'The whole burden will not fall upon you alone, however, for I am arranging for one of our own Women's Social officers, now retired, who is also a trained nurse, to be with us during the day. This will give you some rest and relief, especially as Mrs Coutts needs attention during the night as well.'

Because Mrs Coutts had become increasingly weaker, Lieut-Colonel Joy had virtually taken over the correspondence; and all that Mrs Coutts was required to do was place her signature under the letters. One of the last things she did was sign a batch of letters to a group of retired officers and look at a collection of paintings from one of her grandchildren.

Captain Berner arrived on Monday evening, 11 December. The following morning Mrs Coutts, now very weak, returned home at her own request where Mrs Crate and the captain were waiting to look after her. Captain Berner had decorated the mirror in front of Mrs Coutts' bed.

'Look mother,' said Elizabeth. 'Marianne has put "Welcome home" in little stars.' Mrs Coutts picked up the phrase, but incorrectly, and repeated often to herself: 'Welcome home in the stars. Welcome home in the stars.'

Though deeply concerned about his wife, the General still left for the Westminster Central Hall where the annual carol service was taking place.

That evening Mrs Coutts became unconscious. The doctor advised that her husband should return home immediately and so Elizabeth tried desperately to contact the Central Hall. After much difficulty a message was eventually passed to the General. The General's driver, anticipating the worst, left to make the car ready. Mrs Bessie Coutts died shortly after her husband arrived home.

The funeral service, conducted by the Chief of the Staff, Commissioner Erik Wickberg, took place on Monday morning 18 December, the General requesting that his corps officer read the Scripture portion at the graveside. Because the meeting of remembrance and thanksgiving did not begin until seven o'clock that evening, General Coutts returned to his desk at IHQ where he worked until it was time to leave for the Regent Hall.

Speakers that evening included Songster Leader Douglas Collin, one of her Students' Fellowship members and now a school teacher recently returned from Africa. He referred to Mrs Coutts as the 'mother of students' and 'the only vice-president the international Students' Fellowship has ever had or desired.' Prayer was offered by Lieut-Colonel (Dr) William McAllister whom she had coached when he was a medical student and the Couttses were corps officers in Edinburgh more than thirty years previously.

There was no time for mourning. Within four weeks of the funeral General Coutts was in India and Pakistan. Nothing was cancelled: the traditional Christmas visits to hostels had also been carried out. Amongst several memorials to her name, a holiness table was presented to the corps at St Albans, whilst in Lagos, Nigeria, 'The Mrs General Coutts Memorial Home' for orphan children was opened. Several other territories also opened buildings bearing her name.

Two days after Mrs Coutts death, the General replied to a publisher's request to print his memoirs. He did not feel that his own story could justify that kind of treatment.

'There was a time when I had the leisure to write but since 1953, when I went to our International Training College, whatever may be "creative" in me has had to be harnessed to the task of week by week—and sometimes day by day—addresses in meetings of various kinds. This is even more true now than ever. Were I a Leonard Griffith I might offer you a book of sermons, but my own unprofessional judgment is that there is not a great market nowadays for that kind of production.'

Although accompanied by his daughter, Margaret, it must have been a lonely journey north to Warrington for Frederick Coutts in the summer of 1968 when he was to officially open James Lee House, a social services hostel for men, provided by the borough. It was a great honour that a hostel should bear the name of a bandmaster especially as the suggestion came from the town itself and not from the Army. But that Bessie was not present to honour her father surely made the occasion a supremely sad one for the General. Following Mrs Coutts' promotion to Glory there were to be twenty-one more months of campaigning before he began his round of farewell meetings—alone—just like his welcome.

CHAPTER ELEVEN

A ministry of understanding and encouragement

After more than 2,000 days as General, on 20 September 1969, Frederick Coutts attended his official farewell meeting in the Royal Albert Hall. Appropriately, it featured young people—the group he had always identified himself with so successfully.

At the International College for Officers the principal, Commissioner Olive Gatrall, was preparing to leave for the Albert Hall. Because arrangements were not going smoothly she decided to go on ahead of the delegates so that she would be on time to be seated with the other members of the platform party. On arrival everyone was in place; the meeting was about to begin, but just as she was entering what is known as the 'bull run'—the small passage between the tiered seats on the platform—the General was encountered, standing there alone.

'Good evening, commissioner. How are you?'

'Well, as a matter of fact, I'm feeling rather melancholy,' she replied.

With that he took hold of her arm and drew her to one side: 'I'm going away for a week. When I come back I'll telephone you. I would like us to meet somewhere,' and then looking directly at her, quickly added, 'I mean unofficially.' With that it was time to start the meeting and the commissioner made her way, dazed, onto the platform.

Most of Commissioner Gatrall's officership had been divided between the International Training College, where she was involved in the training of twenty-one sessions and as assistant principal and then as principal of the International College for Officers in which she had taught and influenced fifty-three sessions of officer-delegates. These appointments were punctuated by the seven years she served as private secretary to Mrs General Phillis Orsborn whom she also accompanied on several European tours. Despite the pressure of her appointments she had been the corps cadet guardian at Upper Norwood and had taught in its Sunday-school. She was acknowledged for her skill as a Bible teacher for adults, too. The commissioner sang solos, played the piano and had wide artistic interests. She loved reading and kept a lively interest in Church matters. As principal of the International College she served on the Advisory Council to the General.

Fifteen months after that initial invitation, on the last day of 1970, the General and Commissioner Olive Gatrall were married. They were idyllically happy. During the morning they would share family prayers. The General would read the Scripture portion indicated above the notes in *The Soldier's Armoury,* Mrs Coutts would read the meditation and then the General would read one or two prayers from the BBC publication *New every morning.*

She never knew when he was engaged in his private prayer, he was too reserved a man for that. Prayer was part of his life. His advice was: 'Pray naturally, pray frequently and pray confidently.'

In retirement Coutts had moved back to St Albans into a new house near to where Margaret and her husband Ray lived. His first task was to clear away the bricks and pieces of concrete left behind by the builders. His house was not adorned with the trophies of a world traveller, just a few items here and there decorated his home.

He was glad to have shed the burden of administration and did not hide the fact: 'I am relieved not to be charged any longer with the responsibility of saying who does what and who goes where. Such a duty requires more than the wisdom of Solomon,' he said. 'I thank God for the autumn of life; at least I am alive to savour it,' he confided to retired officers. Neither had he held over any misplaced notions of his self-importance having been crowned with accolade and applause for the past six years. When asked if it was possible to begin to believe all the wonderful things people say of a General when introducing him in a public meeting he replied that it was only the fool who believed them.

His phenomenal memory, with which he could remember the page and paragraph of something he had read, was not only a blessing, but at times a self-confessed curse when he recalled some of the 'daft' things he had said and done in the past.

General Coutts became a loyal soldier at St Albans once more, playing the organ in the meetings. Few things gave him more pleasure than playing the organ whilst his grandson, David, played the piano.

In retirement he remained the student, never wasting a moment, always working on an idea, an article, researching an interesting fact which might be useful in the future. Apart from the constant supply of books he borrowed from the library, his regular diet of reading was the Army press from cover to cover, not only to keep up with things but also for sermon illustrations. Then there were *The Times*, *The Expository Times*, *Radio Times* and Mrs Coutts' *Church Times*. He was lost if he didn't have something in his hands to read—besides he never had any other hobbies.

General and Mrs Coutts' breadth of knowledge and wide interests created stimulating conversations for them in the home—though there were many moments when, present in the flesh, the General's meditations were elsewhere. Mrs Coutts did not intrude on those silences.

'How fortunate is the writer,' said Sir John Hammerton. 'He need never retire.' In retirement, Coutts came to life again creatively. The energy which he had invested in the spoken word during the past sixteen years was now redirected to his writing. His study was a bedroom approximately six metres by four, housing his desk, bookshelves, a cupboard, an old dark brown chest of drawers containing his sermons and several cardboard boxes full of cuttings and scrap books. This was his collectanea; a veritable Alladin's cave for any preacher—for Coutts had started storing up treasure very early in his officership. There was no clue to the uninitiated as to how topics were stored—but there were thousands of quotations.

One Australian officer had commented 'I wish he'd given me the illustrations he threw away.' A set of articles about the Apostles' Creed was pasted into an old cash-book. There were sermons from old religious magazines. One scrap book had been the Expenditure Board Minute Book at the Men's Social Services headquarters; another an old Sunday school register. Other books into which these jewels were set had been purchased at Woolworth's.

There were quotations, interviews and articles from all kinds of writers, on all kinds of subjects, from all kinds of publications. By his desk was a small table at which he typed on an old portable machine whilst seated on a simple wooden kitchen chair. There was no luxury in the room at all. A magnifying glass was now needed to assist with the small print.

There wasn't a book on his shelves which had not been read. The Army books were so well used that their backs were broken. A three-volume Bible dictionary had been used so often that one volume was bound up with pieces of old blue insulating tape, a second with grey insulating tape and a third with black insulating tape.

A set of old encyclopedias, various translations of the Bible and commentaries all showed signs of wear and tear. He had made the contents of his books his own, a principle he taught to others.

In that confined space he produced no fewer than nine books, many demanding enormous research, including volumes six and seven of the official history of The Salvation Army. Other titles included *Bread for my Neighbour* about the social action and influence of William Booth. This was written as a companion to the account of the Army's evangelical growth recorded in *No discharge in this War* and also because social studies were becoming an increasingly important subject in universities, often being read by young salvationists. He hoped that some of the errors existing in prescribed textbooks, especially regarding the work of the Army might then be

177

corrected, not just for the Army's sake, 'but in the interests of students in general'.

Two books of sermons were amongst his publications: *Essentials of Christian Experience* and *In Good Company*, which also included articles from *The Officer*. *The Splendour of Holiness* was a collection of specifically holiness addresses. There was the mammoth task of editing two volumes of *The Armoury Commentary*. The story of Commissioner Gladys Callis inspired him sufficiently to tell her story in *More than one Homeland*. And if he could, he chose a biblical phrase for his chapter headings.

In his younger days he had been a cult figure; in retirement he was an elder-statesman. Soldiers and officers from around the world, and colleagues from former appointments wrote seeking his opinion and advice on theological and scriptural issues, or to ask for information about quotations and matters of Army history and policy. Junior soldiers sent him pictures of themselves in uniform or with news of awards. The reply they received was as attentive as that given to requests from high office. In sensitive and specialist matters his wisdom was sought by International Headquarters. His pen was never still.

He wrote for *The Officer, The War Cry*, the British territory officer magazine *Field Scene*—and he never became tired of the questions. 'I am always glad to have questions from lieutenants,' he wrote. 'It is a sign infallible that they are ticking over on all cylinders—with some, four; with some, six; here and there with all twelve. Keep the engine running!'

The same issues he had written about as 'Ensign' were still actual, but he did not make the mistake of just repeating his earlier conclusions and experiences: 'I am increasingly persuaded that we do not encourage those who are currently bearing the burden and the heat of the day by extolling the past at the expense of the present, as if the present generation were wholly and solely responsible for what, after all, they have only inherited. The truth is that at no time do we need encouragement more than when we are young. . . . At no time are we more capable of responding to encouragement than when we are young.'

And neither could he break the habit of 'specialing' both during the week and on Sundays. With Mrs Coutts he travelled the length and breadth of the United Kingdom. Before setting out he would call in at the field department and enquire if there was anything particular to be noted at the corps. Was the officer ill? How were the children? Were there problems? He still preached in many churches and overseas tours took the Couttses to Belgium, Germany, Australia, America and Canada.

Having accepted an invitation to lead a Bible study and prayer meeting at Crouch End, a small corps in north London, the General was asked to state his travelling expenses. 'I was "specialing" at a large corps last week and I told them I was coming here tonight. I suggested they might like to pay my travelling expenses. Just drop a line to the officer at Wealdstone and thank him, will you?' No corps or setting was too small, no occasion so grand that he would refuse an invitation to preach. And he knew just how to pitch his material to suit his listeners.

He was always popular as a lecturer at the International College for Officers where he would catch the tricky question with: 'Well, thank you, major, for that question.' Then a pause before the measured tread of the first sentence began to be constructed, phrase by phrase. When the full stop was reached this off-the-cuff answer was grammatically correct.

It was on these occasions that he was more than once faced with a questioner who wanted to know if he was a modernist. It had been asked him many times, in many places. Sometimes he would appear a little disturbed by the question, sometimes a little irritated, but the answer was a standard reply: 'Fundamentalist, modernist, the only "-ist" I want to be known by is salvationist.' As testimony to that, in thousands of autograph albums around the Army world stands the line. 'The Salvation Army is the Army for me' signed F. Coutts.

He lectured on a variety of subjects at the ICO, one of

which was concerned with modern theological trends. It began as follows:

> My purpose this morning is much more modest than this high sounding title might suggest. The subject itself was allotted to me some years ago as part of the International College for Officers' curriculum and being, like all of us here present, a man under authority, I had no option but to obey. My purpose is not to attack, or defend any particular school of thought, but merely to try to inform those who, with truly Christian patience, stay tuned throughout the morning. We can do little more than scratch the surface. . . . But I hope we may scratch it together.

His definition of theology was 'but faith thinking aloud. It is faith seeking to give, as we are commanded to be ready to give, a reason for the hope that is in us. . . . What does it mean to be saved? What does it mean to believe? And who is the Lord Jesus Christ that we should believe on him, and how shall we do so? So we need not fear the word theology. Nor fight shy of theological discussion. Differences of opinion are to be preferred to indifference.'

His ICO lectures concerning the doctrine of holiness were a life-changing experience for some delegates. And in this, too, despite a lifetime's study nothing was left to chance. On the first page of his notes was a check list of all the books he needed to take with him.

TAKE
(1)
Handbook of Doctrine
O & R for Officers (Principles)
Chosen to be a soldier
Song Book
New Testament

(2)
BB by C. B.-B
(*Bramwell Booth* by Catherine Bramwell-Booth)
CB by C. B.-B (paperback)

(*Catherine Booth* by same author)
Echoes & Memories
Next to God (*The General next to God*)
History Vol 1
SB Companion (*Companion to the Song Book*)
Sing the Happy Song ch 19, 129-135

And the books were ticked off as assembled, for the lecture in two parts: the first part was concerned with the nature of Christian holiness, and the second concerned with the teaching of the experience. His introduction was written out in full sentences:

> Thank you for your welcome. I appreciate this opportunity given me by the principal for my wife and me to meet you, and this for two reasons. The first is that it is always an enriching experience personally to meet one's comrade officers. . . .
>
> The second is that this morning we are to talk about a personal matter of interest to us all. We each have certain qualifications which fit us for the differing appointments which we hold. In one sense these divide us. For example . . . those of us who are competent to walk a hospital ward may not be so skilled in drawing up a balance sheet.
>
> But when we turn to matters of spiritual welfare, either that of our own or that of our people, as we do when we consider the experience of holiness, then we meet on common ground. This is the concern of us all. When I am asked to speak on the doctrine of holiness then I know I have the interest of you all, whatever your individual appointments may be.

His introduction to the question time was also fully written out.

> You will know that I am retired. I have been retired since 1969—to the consternation of the pension fund board, though I assure you I did not retire until reaching the official age for retirement. Salvation Army officership is too valuable to give away without due cause. But discerning officers who compose this session

will already know that I have no power to promote or demote. After more than sixteen years out of office I have forgotten the drill. Nothing that you say in my hearing or about me can affect your next appointment. Without fear or favour we can proceed with the business in hand.

Other ICO lectures included: 'The atonement'; 'Decision making'; 'The person and work of Christ' and 'The officer and his Bible'.

When challenged about his demanding programme in retirement he answered in a low voice with his eyes towards the ground: 'One must do what one can as long as possible. At my time of life you do not know just how much time is left.'

Coutts' justification for being so deeply interested in Salvation Army history was crystal clear; he wished to pass on that same compulsion, to cadets especially:

> None of us would subscribe to Henry Ford's alleged remark that 'History is bunk'. Though to be fair to him he did explain that history was bunk 'only to me. I did not need it very bad.' But we need it—and need it badly, because without a knowledge of our history, our movement would be both rootless and directionless. We would not know whence we came or whither we were bound. . . . Were I to suffer from loss of memory, I would not be aware of my identity. . . . I would be an 'unperson'.
>
> How can anyone serve the Army as he ought unless he has a reasonably comprehensive and accurate knowledge of the movement to which he has dedicated his life?

What has to be underlined here is that this is not a narrow-minded, bigoted Salvation Army fanatic speaking. This is a man of intellectual standing whose reading and study must probably have been wider than that of any other Salvation Army officer. The man who is saying this has arrived at this position not because he believes someone has to beat the drum, but because a salvationist can understand the present and plan for the future only when he has knowledge of his past. He knew, for instance, that younger officers may only have been aware of the last few Generals and have no adult knowledge of his own term of office. To them William Booth is but 'a legend' and Catherine 'a faint figure indeed'.

Coutts identified two immense areas of ignorance concerning the origin and purpose of the Army. One is among the general public. . . . 'I am continually amazed—and disconcerted—by the ignorance of many in public life who owe it to the office which they hold to know in greater and more current detail about the Army's work.' He cites a British High Commissioner he met in 1964 who thought that 'William Booth was some drunken old reprobate' and a rather important methodist minister with whom he once stayed who had no idea that William Booth had ever had any connection with methodism.

'The other area of ignorance is among our own dear people. Often this is not their fault; it is ours—their appointed teachers. Some of them do not trouble to inform themselves. Others are ignorant because we officers do not teach them. And that does not surprise me when I look at the book cases of some—though happily, not all—which I see in our quarters.'

He believed that a knowledge of Army history would bind the soldiers together, and help them keep their promises. He explained:

> We depend upon the free response of free individuals to further the work of the Army. Much is sometimes made of our multifarious regulations. Their power should not be over-estimated. No one can be compelled to abide by them. Their effectiveness depends upon my free response to them. I cannot be forced to remain an officer or a soldier a moment longer than I wish. The more reason for my knowing the history of the movement in which I serve, and thus recognising that its continuing ideals provide a powerfully compelling motive for remaining within its ranks.

> This is one reason why, since official retirement in 1969, I have been glad to turn my time and attention to Salvation Army history.

Another of his talks in retirement was 'Generals—are they human?' If Coutts was aware of anything, it was that even *Generals* were human. He had heard the first, served under the next six, and worked with four more. He analysed their personalities and achievements and concluded with the sentence: 'For my part I have greatly benefited from each in turn. I have listened and learned, and it is my intention to go on listening and—I hope—learning.'

General Wickberg was gracious towards Coutts and in an informal manner, as colleagues, would speak to him regularly about things happening in the Army world. This contact in no way jeopardised Wickberg's own office or that of the Chief of the Staff. Coutts was always supremely loyal to the Army and especially to the office of the General, even if occasionally in private he disagreed strongly with certain policy decisions.

In February 1981 the Senatus Academicus of the University of Aberdeen announced that it was to confer on General Coutts the degree of Doctor of Divinity *honoris causa*. In July he returned to the city which his father had left in 1887 to become an officer. When presenting Coutts in the beautiful Marischal College, Professor Robin Barbour referred to the General's continual writing and work. 'The books which he has written, both before his retiral and in increasing number since 1969, remind us that we see here a scholar—denied the possibility of taking a university degree—and a man of literary gifts. . . . His books cover all aspects of the Army's faith, life and work, and include volume six of its official history. Himself a scholar, respect for scholarship (not unaccompanied by passing impatience with theological speculation) has characterised all his work. He is a living demonstration of the fact that a clear and informed mind can keep good company with the impassioned heart of the evangelist. . . . Therefore, my Lord Chancellor, I present to you this son of the north-east, this happy warrior, this faithful servant and citizen of the world, this holy and humble man of heart. . . .'

The General's reply, typed on two half A4 sheets of

paper, oblong in format, was timed to meet the requirements of the ceremony. On the two pieces of paper used, there were additions, corrections and amendments in red and black ink. For more than sixty years he had been a public speaker of the highest order and would still leave nothing to chance. Only the finest was good enough:

I am asked to express to the University the thanks of those of us who have shared in today's ceremony, and it seems to this senior citizen that such thanks should take note of two truths which these proceedings have so clearly demonstrated. The first is that this seat of learning turns no blind eye to the manifold activities of our common life. . . . The second is that all of us are beneficiaries of this stimulating diversity, and yet in this fact compelled to recognise anew our basic unity.

The boy who had attended eleven schools in ten years had now been honoured as a scholar.

Coutts had set his heart upon writing the seventh volume of the official history of the Army covering the years between 1946-77. His skills as a writer were not in doubt. His thorough research and absolute faithfulness to the smallest detail were never questioned. However he would be writing about his own period of Generalship and that of two subsequent Generals, Wickberg and Wiseman. Was that not a little too soon? Could a man write objectively a history of his own term of office? The fear was not that he would over-estimate his own work, but that, as in all other matters affecting himself, he would not do himself justice. However, what has been called his 'parting gift' to the Army, *The Weapons of Goodwill*, 347 pages, the seventh volume of the official history of the Army, was given to the movement he served and loved so dearly.

By the time he was finishing the book his life was drawing to a close. It was as if he was driven to finish it, not in a careless hurried fashion, but it had to be completed. Never a day went by without him ringing Major Jenty Fairbank, the Archivist at International Headquarters: 'Coutts here,' was still his introduction.

Sight had gone in one eye and he feared he would lose the sight of the other. Nevertheless he refused any help with the indexing, drawing up the subjects on large sheets of paper headed by the letters of the alphabet. To the end he was independent.

For Frederick Coutts, man and boy, The Salvation Army was his world: a fact that never altered. 'I have never been active in any group or association or fellowship other than the Army. . . . I belong wholly to the Army.' That wholly belonging was born out of his conviction that he belonged fully to Christ: 'He has not only first claim but full claim upon my time and energies. I have no other commitments and am, without reserve, at his disposal.'

*   *   *

January 1986 was a busy month for General Coutts. He was now eighty-six years of age and, within two weeks of that new year breaking, had already conducted two funerals in very bleak weather conditions. On Friday the 17th, Major Fairbank drove him to IHQ with his completed manuscript of volume seven of the Army's official history. But he was still spending long days, tirelessly working on its index.

Sunday evening, 19 January, Frederick Coutts stood to preach in an ecumenical service in the Streatham Baptist Church, on the south side of London. His voice still possessed its resonance and his spirit that peculiar conviction which drew his listeners nearer to Christ. Though no one would have suspected it, this was to be his final public preaching engagement.

The following Tuesday he presented a two-hour lecture on holiness at the International College for Officers. By Saturday the 25th the indexing of 'the history' was complete. The same evening he attended a meeting at St Albans corps where the Sunday-school children were presenting a musical 'Kids' Praise': he always encouraged the young people.

The following Saturday Mrs Coutts had been out collecting for the annual self-denial appeal and to the

Couttses mutual delight the door to door collection had raised more than that of the previous year.

Sunday morning arrived and as usual after breakfast Coutts made his way up to his study to prepare for the meeting. Mrs Coutts heard him call her name. She found him seated at his small table, slightly slumped against the desk on his right. His tunic was hung over the back of the chair, his hands around his cap in which he had placed his sealed cartridge and altar service envelopes. He was not to speak again or regain consciousness before his promotion to Glory four days later from the Mildmay Mission Hospital. It was Thursday 6 February.

*   *   *

Some weeks later a card arrived from the local library saying that a book which Mr Coutts had ordered was now available. Mrs Coutts collected it and upon arriving home took out the baking scales just to see how heavy this tome of Russian literature was. It weighed three-and-a-quarter pounds. He had never stopped learning.

When going through some boxes stored under the stairs Mrs Coutts came across an oil painting, a superb portrait of her husband, which had been presented to him on his world travels whilst General. He had hidden it away as being of no importance. A witty cartoon of himself as a shepherd on a mountain was secured to his desk with a drawing pin, out of sight from others, but serving as a personal reminder for himself of the time he left the literary department to become principal of the International Training College.

It was quite by chance that Mrs Coutts learned shortly before the General's promotion to Glory that the salvationist poet, Peter M. Cooke, was preparing a daily readings book from her husband's writings which had spanned more than sixty years. The General had said nothing to her about the project.

His letters were usually signed with his name only and rarely included his rank: he never sought power nor status. Frederick Coutts remained right to the end of his

187

life a very reserved man. He was uncomfortable being in the limelight and never wished to draw attention to himself in whatever setting. It is perhaps for that reason that, though he had often counselled others at an Army mercy seat, he had never, by his own admission, knelt there in public for himself. He was a very private General indeed.

In 1939, as 'Ensign' in *The Officer*, he wrote of the dangers of disappointment for those who sought power and position:

And what is the conclusion of the matter? Simply that to love God—primarily and absolutely—is the first and greatest commandment of all. . . . The nobler a cause, the greater the opportunities for hypocrisy. We may not even cultivate God's acquaintance in order to be used by him. We are to love him for his own sake, just as if nothing came of it all. Then when we seek first himself, all other things—the increase of those who shall be saved, the progress of our Army, the development of our own powers—shall be added unto us. But his Kingdom—not mine; his power—not mine; his glory—not mine, must come first.

Frederick Coutts was a true salvationist.

Appendix

Written by Frederick Coutts:

The International Company Orders	1937-47
Every man a missionary	c 1940
He had no revolver	1943, 51
I had no revolver	1943
Salute to a mill girl	1942
(four reprints)	
The First Salvationist	1944
(two reprints)	
The Timeless Prophets	1944
Down in Demerara	1944
Half-hours with Heroes	1944
Short measure	1945
The Battle and the Breeze	1946
In the dinner hour	1946
Our Father	1948
The Kingdom of God	1951
Well played!	1953
The Salvationist and his Leisure	1954
Portrait of a Salvationist	1955
The Doctrine of Holiness	1955, 57, 62 & 67
Jesus and our need	1956
The Call to Holiness	1957
Into the Second Century	1965
Are We Great Enough?	1967
Essentials of Christian Experience	1969
The Better Fight	1973
No Discharge in this War	1975
	(copyright 1974)
No Continuing City	1976
Christ is the Answer	1977
Bread for my Neighbour	1978
The Salvation Army in relation to the Church	1978

In Good Company   1981
More than one Homeland   1980
The Splendour of Holiness   1983
The Weapons of Goodwill   1986

Edited by Frederick Coutts:

The Armoury Commentary:
The Four Gospels   1973
The New Testament Epistles   1975

Bessie's father, James Lee, was bandmaster at Warrington for more than forty years

Twelve-year-old Frederick standing next to his mother in a family portrait taken at Warrington before the First World War

Assistant Young People's Sergeant-Major Bessie Lee, BSc (Hons)

The two Coutts boys were very close: Ernest, whose early and tragic death had such a deep impact on Frederick's life, is on the left

Nineteen-year-old Second Lieutenant Frederick Coutts in his Royal Flying Corps uniform

A rare glimpse of Frederick Coutts out of uniform, with John at the top of a French mountain

Commandant and Mrs Coutts, Frederick's parents (right), with women soldiers of the corps at Leith, who produced farthing breakfasts for nearly 300 children each morning in the winters of 1912 and 1913

The young corps officers, Captain and Mrs Coutts, after their marriage in 1925

A happy family at Westcliff-on-Sea just before the Second World War. In the middle are John, Margaret and Molly

Whilst campaigning in New Zealand in 1959, Commissioner Coutts responds to the traditional Maori greeting

When Lieut-Commissioner Coutts was appointed to the International Training College as principal, the cadets soon to arrive were members of the Shepherds' Session. His literary colleagues commissioned and presented him with this Jim Moss cartoon

On the afternoon of their arrival in Sydney, Commissioner and Mrs Coutts were received at Admiralty House by the Governor-General Field Marshal Sir William Slim. Also pictured is Mrs Colonel Herbert Wallace

The General-Elect addresses a company of salvationists which had gathered to meet him at Kingsford Smith Airport, Sydney, upon his return from London

The territorial commander congratulates Sister Ivy Innes upon completing twenty-five years service at territorial headquarters, Sydney

Frederick Coutts often said he was never prouder nor happier than when marching behind an Army flag and in front of a Salvation Army band. He revelled in open-air work as shown here in Port Moresby, Papua New Guinea, in 1960

A fond farewell to Australian salvationists from the decks of the ocean-going liner *Oriana*

The General on his traditional Christmas visit to Army social service centres in the London area

The Chief of the Staff (Commissioner Erik Wickberg) and General Frederick Coutts formed an impressive partnership in the annals of Salvation Army leadership

At press conferences, the General always carefully considered the questions before replying

Commissioner Frederick Coutts about to sign the deed of acceptance as the eighth General of The Salvation Army following his election at Sunbury Court on 1 October 1963

General Frederick Coutts preaching to more than 10,000 people in the cathedral church of St John the Divine in New York, as part of the Army's centenary celebrations in the United States, in 1965

A high point in Salvation Army history was when, in 1965, HM Queen Elizabeth II attended the opening ceremony of the Army's centenary celebrations in the Royal Albert Hall. The Archbishop of Canterbury, Dr Michael Ramsey, can be seen on the right of the picture

Her Majesty Queen Elizabeth II opens the new men's social services centre at Booth House in East London, one of a number of centenary projects

During the centenary celebrations Commissioner W. Wycliffe Booth unveils a memorial plaque to his grandfather William Booth in Westminster Abbey. The Dean of Westminster, Dr Eric S. Abbott, looks on

General Coutts is received by one of East Africa's first national leaders, President Jomo Kenyatta

General Coutts in discussion with the Mayor of Hiroshima

Coutts, the man of peace, did not express his feelings to anyone when visiting Hiroshima's Peace Park where he laid a wreath

Preaching the word in Kinshasa, the Congo, in September 1964

Escorted by Militia Guards, General Coutts enters the João Caetano Theatre for a music festival whilst on tour in Brazil, in 1967

The international leader being escorted by the Mayor of Madras to a civic reception

Ever the internationalist, General Coutts always enjoyed his contacts at the International College for Officers—the Cedars in South London—where he lectured on a variety of subjects

The Most Reverend Iakouos, Archbishop of the Greek Orthodox Church of North and South America, and a President of the World Council of Churches, in conversation with Commissioner Holland French and General Coutts, in New York

On overseas tours, a General always has to make time for the photo-call

General Coutts sharing a platform with Dr Billy Graham and singers Cliff Richard and Beverly Shea

The General and the Archbishop of Westminster, Cardinal John Heenan, at a reception in London

The Rev Dr Laton E. Holmgren, a general secretary of the American Bible Society, presents a copy of the Bible to General Coutts

At bandmasters' councils, held at the
William Booth Memorial Training
College, Denmark Hill, General Coutts
talks to Bandmaster Gordon Hughes,
of Warrington

General Coutts with two of his
greatest joys in life: a piano and a
group of young people

In the summer of 1967, Mrs General Bessie Coutts made her final public appearance during congress meetings in Finland when this photograph was taken

On the last day of 1970, the General and Commissioner Olive Gatrall were married in a ceremony conducted by General Erik Wickberg

In 1980, the Literary Secretary (Lieut-Colonel Walter Hull) (left) presented the Chief of the Staff (Commissioner Stanley Cottrill) (right) with copies of General Coutts' latest book In Good Company.

When travelling 'north of the border', Frederick Coutts always made the most of his Scottish nationality. It was a special honour for him, in May 1965, to be admitted as a 'guild brother, burgess and freeman of the Royal Burgh of Kirkcaldy', his birthplace

Margaret (left) and Elizabeth (right) accompanied their father to Buckingham Palace when he was created a Commander of the Order of the British Empire (CBE). Margaret's sons, Andrew (left) and David, also offered their support on the big day